The Hye Ch'o Diary

RELIGIONS OF ASIA SERIES

Number 2

Editors

Lewis R. Lancaster
(*University of California, Berkeley*)

and

J. L. Shastri
(*M. P. Education Service, RTD.*)

The Hye Ch'o Diary:

Memoir of the Pilgrimage to the Five Regions of India

Translation, text and editing by:
YANG, HAN-SUNG
JAN, YÜN-HUA
and
IIDA, SHOTARO
LAURENCE W. PRESTON

Asian Humanities Press
Po Chin Chai Ltd.

Printed in Korea

Published by Asian Humanities Press P. O. Box 3056 Berkeley, California 94703 and Po Chin Chai Ltd. 8-5 Ga Dangsan-Dong Yeongdeungpo-Ku Seoul, Korea

UNESCO COLLECTION OF REPRESENTATIVE WORKS
Published with the agreement of the Republic of Korea

ISBN 0 89581 0247

CONTENTS

Plates		
Acknowledgements		
Editors' Preface		1
Part I	Buddhist Pilgrims	5
Part II	Translation of *Memoir of a Pilgrimage to the Five Regions of India*	37
Part III	Manuscript and Edition	75
Index		115

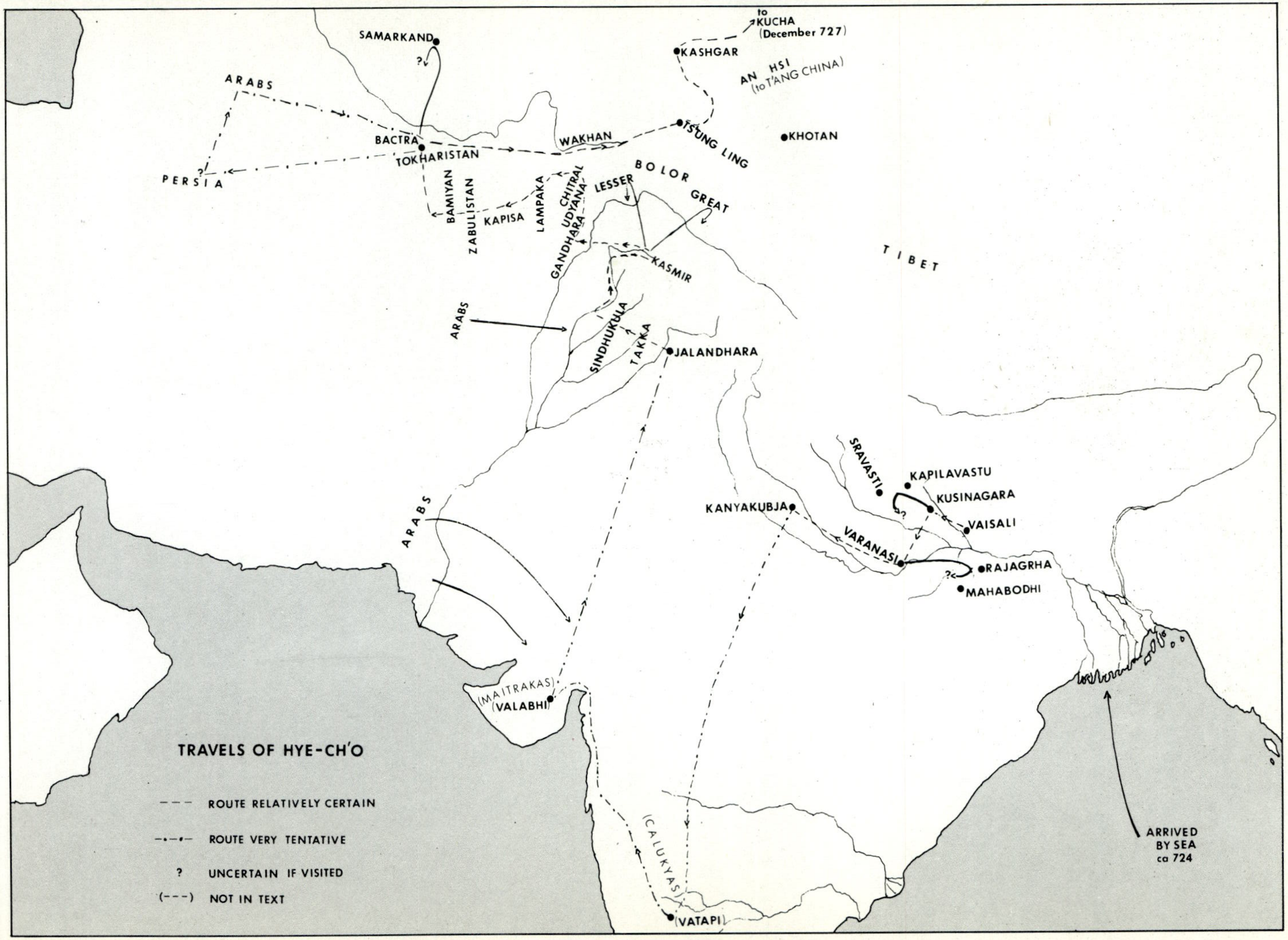
TRAVELS OF HYE-CH'O
ROUTE RELATIVELY CERTAIN
ROUTE VERY TENTATIVE
? UNCERTAIN IF VISITED
(---) NOT IN TEXT
to KUCHA (December 727)
KASHGAR
AN HSI (to T'ANG CHINA)
SAMARKAND
ARABS
BACTRA
TOKHARISTAN
WAKHAN
TSUNG LING
KHOTAN
PERSIA
BAMIYAN
ZABULISTAN
KAPISA
LAMPAKA
CHITRAL
UDYANA
GANDHARA
LESSER
BOLOR
GREAT
KASMIR
TIBET
ARABS
SINDHUKULA
TAKKA
JALANDHARA
ARABS
SRAVASTI
KAPILAVASTU
KUSINAGARA
VAISALI
KANYAKUBJA
VARANASI
RAJAGRHA
MAHABODHI
(MAITRAKAS)
(VALABHI)
(CALUKYAS)
(VATAPI)
ARRIVED BY SEA ca 724

Entrance to Cave 17 at Tun-huang in west China where the diary of Hye Ch'o was disovered in 1908 by Paul Pelliot.

← From India through Central Asia and across north China, great cave complexes were constructed to serve as religious centers. One of the most important of these caves are the several hundred which line the cliffs at an oasis spot at Tun-huang. Today, the desert constantly threatens to engulf the famous caves which are filled with treasures in the form of paintings and images that have survived through the centuries.

Photos by Lois Lancaster

Stūpas still mark the Silk Road route taken by merchants and pilgrims on their way West, going toward Rome or India.

ACKNOWLEDGEMENTS

I wish to record my thanks to Dr. K. M. Varma of India, who has kindly sent me the Fuchs, German translation from Berlin when he was in Germany; also Dr. Walter Fuchs of Germany, Professor Koh Byong-ik of Korea and Professor J. Sram of Czechoslovakia for their encouragement and help in my translation of Hye Ch'o's *Memoirs,* and to my secretary, Mrs. Grace Gordon, who has kindly typed the manuscript of my translations, as well as other articles relevant to this project during the last six years.

JAN Yün-hua
Professor,
Department of Religion,
McMaster University,
Hamilton, Ontario, Canada.

We wish to acknowledge our debt to Mr. Yim Tse, Librarian of the Asian Studies Library, University of British Columbia, who has very generously and patiently spent countless hours going through readings which many have previously found difficult and uncertain. In addition, we would like to thank Dr. Jennifer Jay-Preston for her help in historical continuity in the translation. Without the help of these two, the editorial work would certainly not have been as accurate as it is. Needless to say, all remaining errors are the responsibility of the editors.

Iida, Shotaro
Associate Professor
Department of Religious Studies
University of British Columbia
Vancouver, B, C. CANADA

Laurence W. Preston
Ph. D. Candidate
Department of History
University of Toronto
Ontario, CANADA

EDITORS' PREFACE

The travels of a little known eighth-century Korean monk would probably have escaped any notice had it not been for the discovery of a manuscript at Tun-huang in 1908 by Paul Pelliot. It is to that eminent scholar that must go the initial credit for this translation of Hye Ch'o's *Memoir of a Pilgrimage to the Five Regions of India*. It is surprising that, except for an obscure German translation by W. Fuchs, Hye Ch'o's *Memoir* should have remained so little known in this century after the discovery of the manuscript by Pelliot. Hye Ch'o's *Memoir* is a contemporary witness of eighth-century India, the type of personal account so lacking in ancient Indian history. The *Memoir* is an important addition to the Chinese Buddhist Pilgrims' writings on India, as exemplified by Fa-hsien and Hsüan-tsang. Hye-Ch'o is also perhaps unique in that he was of Korean origin Kim (Hui Ch'ao); his *Memoir* attests to the brotherhood felt amongst even the extremities of the Buddhist world of his time. The difficulties of travel in Asia in the eighth century were immense, as Hye Ch'o describes in his poetry. Yet, men like Hye Ch'o would endure these hardships in order to visit the holy sites of the Buddhist world. His *Memoir* is then in part a record of the unifying cultural force of Buddhism in Asia.

The editors of this translation learned that two scholars working independently had developed an interest in Hye Ch'o and were preparing English translations of his *Memoir*. We decided that the efforts of these two scholars should be combined so that a standard first English translation of this work could be published. The translation of Professor Han Sung Yang, formerly of Hanyang University, came to the notice of the editors through the good offices of Dr. Lewis Lancaster of the University of California at Berkeley. The editors also learned that Dr. Yün hua Jan of MacMaster University, who has published several articles on Hye Ch'o, had readied his translation of the *Memoir*. The editors were also aware that a Japanese translation of the *Memoir* had been recently published by Professor Sadakata Akira of Japan. The editors were able to draw on the hard labours of these scholars to produce what we believe is the most accurate and consistent rendering of a difficult manuscript into readable English.

The duties of the editors were twofold. Firstly, by comparison of the available translations many points of discrepancy were discovered.

Dr. Shotaro Iida, the general editor of this translation, undertook the linguistic analysis of the particular points of difficulty. The language of Hye Ch'o is in many places quite obscure. The editors have decided upon the most logically consistent, (common sense) translation of these difficult points. The extensive footnotes, prepared by Professor Yang and Dr. Iida, refer to these difficult points in the text. The second duty of the editors was to render Hye Ch'o's *Memoir* into English in a style both readable and appropriate to a historical narrative. This duty, along with the preparation of an introduction, was undertaken by Laurence Preston. The first translation of any ancient manuscript is always difficult, particularly so in the translation of ancient Chinese records of foreign lands. The editors sincerely hope that their year of labour, even for a text the length of this *Memoir*, will justify the many years work of the translators.

Perhaps the greatest story of intellectual and spiritual intercourse between two great world cultures was that of the introduction and development of Buddhism from India to China. Here were two mature cultures, separated by immense physical, linguistic and cultural factors, yet, starting from the early centuries of the Christian era, Buddhism left India, travelled the hazardous tracks of Central Asia and of the Southern oceans, and became established as an integral part of Chinese culture. Buddhism must certainly be the most important and profound doctrine ever to be accepted by the Chinese from outside their own culture. Buddhism must certainly also be the most important and lasting doctrine which India gave to Asia. In Asia, the history of Buddhism is the history of contact between cultures. Thus, when Buddhism was alive in India, Chinese culture was in direct contact with Indian culture.

While China adopted Buddhism, an Indian religion, it is true to say that China adapted and assimilated Buddhism. Buddhism responded to the culture it found itself in wherever it went in Asia. In China, the classical civilization, particularly Taoist philosophy, molded Buddhism into an integral part of Chinese civilization and history. After Buddhism declined in India after 1000 A. D., the basic storehouse of Indian Buddhist thought was exhausted. Chinese Buddhism then developed within itself, it in fact became Chinese.

However, while Buddhism was alive and developing in India, China was very conscious of Buddhism's Indian origins. India was the center of orthodoxy. India was the home of the most sacred Buddhist pilgrimage sites, it was the land where Buddha had lived and taught. The sacred books of Buddhism were written in Indian languages and had to be translated into Chinese. The great masters and commentators of Buddhism lived and worked in India, where the most famous Buddhist institutions of learning were located. It is no wonder then, that there should arise the desire among Chinese Buddhists to go to India, to visit the sacred spots, to search for Buddhist books and to learn the Indian languages. Buddhism had entered China with merchants along the trade routes, the early translations of the canonical books had been difficult, done through many intermediaries. The introduction of Buddhism to China was not in the nature of an organized missionary activity, thus China received many confused parts of the whole religion. In addition, at this time Buddhism in India was undergoing many profound changes. For example, Mahayana doctrines were developing at the very time Buddhism first entered China. For these reasons, there was the desire to go to India to study the traditions, doctrines and disciplines of Buddhism at first hand so that China could have a systematic account of Buddha's teaching and its subsequent developments.

From the second to tenth centuries A.D. many Chinese Buddhist monks made the long journey to India. Most of these are unknown to us except perhaps for a brief notice. There were, however, some of these pilgrims who wrote accounts of their journey to India. Thus we are fortunate in having several accounts, spread over the centuries of the first millenium A. D., of Chinese Buddhist pilgrims' journeys to India. Each of these accounts possesses an intrinsic interest and value. There are elements in the various accounts which compliment each other and there are elements which each pilgrim develops individually. While recording what particularly interested them (for we must remember that the accounts were written by Buddhist pilgrims for an audience interested in a very foreign but sacred land), the accounts also give the modern reader much important historical and social information. Because the accounts were written by Buddhist pilgrims we are also given a valuable and imcomparable insight into the contemporary state of the Buddhist religion, which was the intellectual and spiritual environment during the period of the most profound contact between the two great ancient Asian cultures, India and China.

The following are brief biographies of the pilgrims in which we are most interested.

Part I

Buddhist Pilgrims

Fa-hsien

The first Buddhist pilgrim who has left an account of his travels was the monk Fa-hsien. In his small work, Fa-hsien has recorded his travels to Central Asia, India and Ceylon. Fa-hsien was a native of Shan-si; he left home at three years of age to join the Buddhist Sangha. After his noviciate, Fa-hsien developed the desire to go to India to search for books of the *vinaya piṭaka,* the monastic rules of Buddhism. Fa-hsien was perhaps twenty-five years of age when, in 399 A. D., he departed for India. The record states that

> Fa-hsien had been living in Ch'ang-an. Deploring the mutilated and imperfect state of the collection of the Books of Discipline [*Vinaya piṭaka*], in the second year of the period *Hwang-che,* being the *Ke-hae* year of the cycle (399 A. D.), he entered into an engagement with Hui-ching Tao-ching, Hui-ying and Hui-wei, that they should go to India and seek for the Disciplinary rules.[1]

Fa-hsien undertook the dangerous journey through the deserts of Central Asia and across the Pamir and Hindu Kush mountains to reach India. Much courage and determination was required by the pilgrims to make this journey. Throughout his travels, Fa-hsien constantly displayed such courage. Fa-hsien records that in the deserts,

> ... there are many evil demons and hot winds. (Travellers) who encounter them perish all to a man. There is not a bird to be seen in the air above, nor an animal on the ground below. Though you look all round most earnestly to find where you can cross, you know not where to make your choice, the only mark and indication being the dry bones of the dead (left upon the sand).[2]

Fa-hsien travelled in northern India, visiting the holy Buddhist sites located in the valley of the Ganges river. Kapilavastu, the place of Buddha's birth; Bodhgayā, the site of Buddha's enlightenment; Sārnāth, where Buddha preached his first sermon; and Kuśingara, the place of Buddha's death and final liberation were among the sites Fa-hsien and the other pilgrims visited and described. In the accounts of the other pilgrims most parts of India and Central Asia were at one time visited and described. Fa-hsien however, after travelling through Central Asia and North West India, spent much of his time visiting and describing mid-India or Magadha, the homeland of the Buddha. Fa-hsien did not visit peninsular or South India. Fa-hsien left India by sea to return to China. He did however visit Ceylon on his return voyage. This is the only first-hand account of that important Buddhist island from a Chinese Buddhist pilgrim. Fa-hsien returned to China in 414 A. D. after enduring many hardships at sea. At one point he encountered a severe storm, at another he was in danger of being marooned by the crew of the ship in which he was travelling. Fa-hsien's journey is summarized in the following way,

> After Fa-hsien set out from Ch'ang-an it took him six years to reach Central India; stoppages there extended over (another) six years; and on his return it took him three years to reach Ch'ing-chou. The countries through which he passed were a few under thirty. From the sandy desert westward on to India, the beauty of the dignified demeanour of monkhood and of the transforming influence of the Law was beyond the power of language fully to describe; and reflecting how our masters had not heard any complete account of them, he therefore (went on) without regarding his own poor life or (the dangers to be encountered) on the sea upon his return, thus incurring hardships and difficulties in a double form. He was fortunate enough, through the dread power of the three Honoured Ones, to receive help and protection in his perils; and therefore he wrote out an account of his experiences, that worthy readers might share with him in what he heard and said.[3]

Sung Yün and Hui Sheng

Sung Yün and Hui-sheng were despatched in 518 A. D. as an embassy to the western countries by the Empress Dowager Ta-hao of the so-called Great Wei dynasty, a dynasty of invading peoples known as the T'o-pa. The pilgrims' object was to obtain Buddhist books, of which they returned with 170 volumes belonging to the Mahayana persuasion. Sung Yün was probably considered well suited to undertake such an expedition because he was a native of Tun-huang, located at the Chinese Central Asian frontier. Tun-huang was the Chinese terminus of the southern trade route through Central Asia. Perhaps for this reason Sung Yün travelled from China to India by the southern route via Khotan.

Sung Yün and Hui-sheng did not visit mid-India, they reached only Gandhāra at about the present day Peshawar. The pilgrims were well received when they reached Udyāna, around the present day Swāt valley. It is reported that,

> The king of the country seeing Sung Yün (inquired respecting him, and) on their saying that the ambassadors of the Great Wei (dynasty) had come, he courteously received their letters of introduction. On understanding that the Empress Dowager was devotedly attached to the law of Buddha, he immediatly turned his face to the east, and, with closed hands and meditative heart, bowed his head; then, sending for a man who-could interpret the Wei language, he questioned Sung Yün and said, "Are my honourable visitors men from the region of sunrising?" Sung Yün answered and said," Our country is bounded on the east by the great sea; from this the sun rises according to the divine will (the command of the Tathāgata).[4]

However, Sung Yün and Hui-sheng found their reception in Gandhāra less than warm, for when they met the king of Gandhāra,

> Sung Yün repaired to the royal camp to deliver his credentials. The king was very rough to him, and failed to salute him. He sat whilst receiving the letters. Sung Yün perceived that these remote barbarians were unfit for excercising public duties, and that their arrogancy refused to be checked.[5]

Northwest India was in a state of political unrest during the period of Sung Yün's travels. It would appear that for this reason, as seen in the unfriendly actions of the king of Gandhāra, the pilgrims were unable to proceed further than the Indus river to the holy Buddhist pilgrimage sites. The object of their travels, to obtain Buddhist books, being achieved, the pilgrims returned to China in 521 A. D.

Hsüan-tsang

The most renowned of Chinese Buddhist Pilgrims was the Master of the Law Hsüan–tsang. Hsüan–Tsang was born in Ho-nan in 603 A. D. In early life, Hsüan–tsang displayed obvious signs of intellectual and spiritual greatness. Even at an early age, Hui–li, Hsüan–tsang's biographer reports that,

> ... he, Hsüan–tsang, took to reading the sacred books [Chinese Classics], and was charmed with the writings of the ancient sages. A book without elegance and propriety he would not look at; he would have not intercourse with those who were opposed to the holy and wise...[6]

Hsüan–tsang left home at a very early age, entered the Buddhist monkhood at the age of thirteen while residing in the city of Lo–yang. Hui–li says that,

> His second brother Chang–tsi had previously become a disciple of Buddha, and dwelt in the convent of Ching–tu at Lo–yang. Observing that the Master of the Law was deeply given to the study of religious doctrine, he therefore took him to his convent and taught him the method and practice of the sacred sooks (of Buddhism).[7]

Due to the political and social unrest caused by the fall of the Sui dynasty, Hsüan–tsang went to Hsing–tu in Szechuan, where he was ordained at the age of twenty. From here, Hsüan–tsang travelled throughout China in search of knowledge of the sacred books of the Buddhists. At length, he came to Ch'ang–an, then under the peaceful rule of the T'ang emperor T'ai–tsung. It was here, Hsüan–tsang developed the desire to visit India. Hui–li reports that,

> The Master of the Law, having visited the celebrated Masters all round, devoured their words and examined their principles; and so he found that each followed implicitly the teaching of his own school; but on verifying their doctrine he saw that the holy books differed much, so that he knew not which to follow. He then resolved to travel to the Western world in order to ask about doubtful passages.[8]

Hsüan–tsang was conscious of the example of Fa–hsien before him. Like Fa–hsien, Hsüan–tsang was concerned about the incomplete and misinterpreted nature of the Buddhist scriptures that reached China. The introduction of Chang–yueh to Hsüan–tsang's record summarizes this idea common among the Chinese Buddhist Pilgrims when it says,

> Now Buddha having been born in the Western region and his religion

> having spread eastwards, the sounds of the words translated have been often mistaken, the phrases of the different regions have been misunderstood on account of the wrong sounds, and thus the sense has been lost. The words being wrong, the idea has been perverted.[9]

The work Hsüan-tsang has left us, the *Hsi-yü chi* is the longest and most detailed account of the countries of Central Asia and India we possess by a Chinese Buddhist Pilgrim. While Hsüan-tsang's purpose was to obtain Buddhist books and to receive instruction while in India, he did more, as the introduction to his records says,

> ...after he (Hsüan–tsang) had travelled afar in search of the law, in his moments of leisure he has preserved these records of the character of the lands (visited).[10]

Hsüan-tsang obtained and translated 657 Sanskrit Buddhist works as well as receiving the best instruction he could find throughout India. Much of this activity is detailed in the *Hsi-yü chi* companion volume, the biography of Hsüan-tsang by Hui-li. However, Hsüan-tsang in his records, as the Preface to the *Hsi-yü chi* by Chang-yueh states,

> . . . thoroughly examined the different manners of distant countries, the diverse customs of separate people, the various products of the soil and the class divisions of the people, the regions where the royal calendar is received and where the sounds of moral instruction [of Buddhism] have come, he has composed in twelve books the *Ta-T'ang Hsi-yu chi* [the records of the Western regions during the Great T'ang dynasty].[11]

Hsüan-tsang travelled from China in 629 A. D. through Central Asia by the northern trade route via Kucha, and reached Northern India, where he was the guest of the great Indian emperor at the city of Kanauj. He visited the sacred Buddhist sites in Magadha and spent much time studying at the great Nālanda monastery, then the center of Buddhist scholarship. The pilgrim then travelled to South and West India. He returned to China, again by way of Central Asia, though this time by the southern trade route via Khotan. Hsüan-tsang recorded the details of all the countries he visited. He also included information on countries he had heard reports of; for example, he was able to record some stories concerning Ceylon when he was in South India, though he had not visited the island. Hsüan-tsang returned to China in 645 A. D. He was accorded much esteem on his return, but refused all high civil appointments offered by the still-reigning emperor, Tai-Tsung. Hsüan-tsang retired to a monastery devoting his labours to translating Buddhist texts until his death in 664 A. D.

I-ching

While Hsüan-tsang was in India, there was born, near present day Peking, the next pilgrim to leave an account of his travels to India. I-ching was seven years old when be began a secular education.

His teacher died when he was twelve years old. When I-ching tells us that,

> Laying aside my study of secular literature, I devoted myself to the Sacred (Buddhist) Canon. In my fourteenth year [648] I was admitted to the Order, and it was in my eighteenth year [652] that I formed the intention of travelling to India, which was not, however, realized till my thirty-seventh year. [671].[12]

After his ordination in 654 A. D., I-ching spent five years in the study of the *Vinaya piṭaka*. The rules of discipline were to remain I-ching's main interest and they form the main topic of his records. The pilgrim spent several years studying the *Abhidharma* literature. He was aware of the travels of Fa-hsien and also of the immediate example of Hsüan-tsang, when he formed his desire to go to India. I- ching and Hsüan-tsang were, in fact, contemporaries. I- ching was staying at Ch'ang-an when Hsüan-tsang's funeral took place there in 664 A. D.

I-ching left China for India from Canton by the sea route. arriving in India in 673 A. D. After visiting the sacred Buddhist sites in Magadha, he resided for ten years (676–685) at the great Nālanda monastery, where he devoted himself to the study of the *Vinaya*. I-ching left India in 685 A. D. for the city of Bhoja, perhaps located on the island of Sumatra, which at this time was very much under the cultural influence of India. Here he devoted himself to the translation of Buddhist Sanskrit texts, particularly the *Vinaya* of the Mūlasarvāstivādin school. In 689 A. D., I- ching returned to China to obtain assistants for his translations. He then returned to Bhoja where he remained for five more years, returning to China in 695 A.D., during the reign of the well-known patron of Buddhism, the Empress Wu. He received much acclaim on his return, but like his predecessor Hsüan-tsang, I-ching devoted the remaining years of his life to the translation of Buddhist works. He died in 713 A. D. at the age of 79, during the reign of the Emperor Chung-tsung.

Apart from his translations, I-ching left two important works. The *Ch'iu-fa kao-seng chuan* is a series of brief biographies of Chinese Buddhist pilgrims that he met or heard of while he was in India. This work is interesting in that it gives an impression of the numbers of pilgrims who went to India but have left no records of their own. His major work, the *Nan-hai chi-kuei nei-fa chuan* or *A Record of the Buddhist Religion Sent Home from the Southern Sea,* is quite unique among the records left by the Buddhist pilgrims. Perhaps because of the monumental *Hsi-yü chi* of Hsüan-tsang, I-ching did not attempt to describe the country of India. In any case, his travels were in themselves quite limited. He did, however, describe the Buddhist practices in India of what he considered to be the orthodox interpretation of the *Vinaya.* As he states,

> . . . on account of some misinterpretations handed down, the disciplinary rules have suffered, and errors constantly repeated have become customs which are contrary to the original principles. Therefore, according to the noble teaching and the principal customs actually carried on in India, I have carefully written the the following articles which are forty in number and have divided them into four books.[13]

Hye Ch'o(Hui Ch'ao)[14]

Since the discovery of the fragmentary manuscript of Hye Ch'o's *Memoir of a Pilgrimage to the Five Regions of India,* by Paul Pelliot at Tun-huang in 1908,[15] various attempts have been made to study Hye Ch'o's life and works.[16] Scholars have already arrived at certain conclusions, yet many points remain to be recorded and discussed. With the foundation of earlier research, we are in a better position today to evaluate the life and works of this eminent Korean monk and pilgrim. As no biography of Hye Ch'o exists in the collections of monks in Chinese, we have first attempted a comprehensive account of life. Further, an assessment of some important points in Hye Ch'o's memoir has been presented with a view to emphasizing the importance of this memoir for students of the eighth century Asian history.

Hye Ch'o was a native of Hsin-lo, or the Kingdom of Silla, in the Korean peninsula. This is clearly indicated in his writings, and can be re-affirmed from other sources.[17] Our sources do not record whether Hye Ch'o was born in Silla proper or in China. Our sources do not, likewise, record the date of his birth. If we are to judge from the apparent time of his death,[18] a date around 700 A. D. would appear likely for his birth. Some scholars have suggested Hye Ch'o was born in 704 A. D. or 1364 of the Buddhist era.[19] This date has been based on the assumption that he in fact met and became a disciple of Vajrabodhi (671–741 A. D.), a celebrated master of Tantric Buddhism.[20] Vajrabodhi arrived at Kuang-chou (Canton) in South China in 719 A. D., where it is supposed he met Hye Ch'o when the latter was a sixteen year-old youth. While this suggestion seems reasonable, Hye Ch'o was soon after to leave on his pilgrimage from South China and there is no original evidence to support this supposition.

Our sources do not give any details of Hye Ch'o's early life.[21] While the extant manuscript of Hye Ch'o's *Memoir* is missing the first section relating to his journey from China, the place and time of the pilgrim's departure can be reconstructed. He left sometime shortly before 724. This date has been deduced as the date of the commencement of the extant manuscript at Kuśinagara, near Vārānasī, by calculating the number of days moving backwards from the date of December 727 A. D. that he gives for his arrival at An-hsi in Chinese territory.[22] Hye Ch'o made his departure from South China and travelled by the southern sea route to India, much as his predecessor I- ching had done. The initial part of Hye Ch'o's pilgrimage can be ascertained from quotations made by Hui-lin (737–820) from the full text of Hye Ch'o's *Memoir*. In these quotations there are certain geographical and anthropological names such as *Kao-mieh* (Khmer), *Po-ti, Lo-hsing-kuo* or the Island of Naked people (Nicobar) etc., which clearly indicate the pilgrim's route to India.[23]

Hye Ch'o's travels in India commenced when he landed in the eastern part of the country, as is clearly seen in the quotations used by Hui-lin.[24] Hye-Ch'o records in his *Memoir* that he made pilgrimages to holy sites such as Sārnāth, Kuśinagara, Rājagṛha and Bodhgayā. He also visited cities such as Vārāṇasī and Kanauj. From North-central India, he went to the south, to the capital of what has been identified at the Chalukya kingdom.[25] Later he continued his travels and came to Western India, which has been identified as the Valabhī kingdom of the Kathiawar peninsula.[26] Hye Ch'o then travelled to North-west India, by way of the city of Jālandhara and visited the kingdoms lying on the banks of the Indus. He went further north to the Kaśmīr valley and its neighboring countries. After passing through the lands of Gandhāra, Kāpiśa and a number of Central Asian states, he finally arrived at An-hsi, the frontier city of the T'ang empire, which is identified by Hye Ch'o himself as Kucha. The manuscript records that he arrived at An-hsi in the eleventh moon of the fifteen year of the K'ai-yuan era, *i. e.* December 727.[27]

After his return to China from India, Hye Ch'o probably resided at Ch'ang-an in the Ta chien-fu monastery and worked under Vajrabodhi. The source for Hye Ch'o's association with Vajrabodhi is from the preface to the *Mahāyāna-yogavajra-prakṛtisāgara-manjuśrī-sahasrabāhu-sahasrapatra-mahātantrarāja-sūtra.* This preface states that Hye Ch'o began the study of this *sūtra* on the 21st of January, 733 *i.e.* the seventh day of the 21st year of the K'ai-yuan era. The same source also records that after eight years of study, the translation of the *sūtra* was inaugurated by Vajrabodhi on Janurary 6, 741. Hye ch'o was the assistant translator (*pei-shu*) or scribe.[28] Unfortunately, before the completion of the translation, the project was suspended on the death of Vajrabodhi, who passed away during the autumn of 741. Subsequently, under Vajrabodhi's last testament, the original Sanksrit manuscript of the *sūtra* was sent back to India on March 30,742. The preface also states that following the death of Vajrabodhi, Hye Ch'o studied the later part of the *sūtra* under the guidance of Amoghavajra (705–774 A. D.) during the months November/December 774. Afterwards, on May 23, 780, Hye Ch'o took the translation to the Wu-t'ai Mountain to be copied. The copying started June 11 of the same year at the Ch'ien-yuan P'u-t'i Monastery.

Hye Ch'o's association with Vajrabodhi is solely dependent on the preface to this *sūtra,* the translation into Chinese of which is attributed to Amoghavajra.[29] The authenticity of this translation and particularly of the preface, however, has become a matter of some controversy. While previously this work has been accepted by scholars and catalogu-ers as a genuine work of Amoghavajra, recent studies have challenged this unqualified acceptance.[30]

According to some scholars, the *sūtra* and its preface are apocry-phal. The questions raised and the evidence put forward by these scholars include:

1. Vajrabodhi died in the month September/October 741; thus how could he instruct his followers to return the original Sanskrit manusript of the *sūtra* to India in the year 742?[31]
2. Amoghavajra passed away on July 28, 774.; thus, how could he teach the later part of the *sūtra* to Hye Ch'o in the month of November/Decem-ber of the same years?[32]
3. If the *sūtra* had been completed in 780, why was it not included in two comtemporary works, *the Chen-yüan shih-chiao lu* (A Catalogue of Buddhist Literature compiled during the age of Chen-yüan) and *Yi-ch'ieh-ching yin-yi* (A Comprehensive Dictionary of Canons) compiled in the years 800 and 807, respectively.[33]
4. Moreover, according to an early source, when Vajrabodhi went to China he lost all of his Sanskrit manuscripts, so how could he retain this *sutra* and transmit it to Hye Ch'o?[34]
5. The writing and style of presentation of the *sūtra* appears very much influenced by exegetic techniques and its contents have a strong flavor of Pure Land Buddhism. As the work was first found in the collection of a monastery at the Wu-t'ai Mountain by the monk Heng-an in 938,[35] it is, therefore, perhaps a Chinese compilation done during the latter part of the T'ang period (*circa* 9th century). Some scholars have even quoted passages from this *sūtra* and compared them with parallel passa-ges existing in the *Fan-wang-ching* and thus have concluded that it is nothing more than a commentary or annotation of the *Chin-kang-ting-ching Ta-yü-chia Hsin-ti fa-men yi-chüeh* by Amoghavajra.[36]

While these points are worth consideration, the information given in the preface to the *sūtra* cannot be totally dismissed without further examination. Even scholars who have challenged the authenticity of the translation have had to accept the details of the life of Hye Ch'o supplied by the preface.[37] We would venture to suggest that the preface and *sūtra,* though they may be the words of a later compiler, might be based on an unfinished manuscript originally handed down from Hye Ch'o[38]

With regard to the internal discrepancies over dating, it should be noted that in the preface two methods have been used to record dates. The first recorded dates together with the cyclical characters. For example, the preface states,

> In the twenty-first year of the K'ai-yuan age, the cyclical order of the year was Kuei-yu.[39]

In another place the preface again states,

> In the twenty-eighth year of the K'ai-yuan age the cyclical order of the year was Keng-shen.[40]

To record dates along with their cyclical characters was the traditional method used by Chinese historians. To calculate and identify the cyclical characters with the corresponding dates was not an easy task. Even some eminent Buddhist historians have made mistakes about the cyclical characters of medieval times.[40a] At least in the two instances cited above, the dates are quite correct and identical with the related historical dates. This tends to prove that the two dates shown above were written during the life of Hye Ch'o or were at least based on a contemporary record of the events.

This method of recording dates, however, is found only in the first part of the preface. Thereafter, dates are recorded without reference to their cyclical characters. The important point is that the dates which have raised controversies among scholars all belong to this second part of the preface. The differences between these two historiographic methods used in the same preface are very significant. We conclude, that the dates recorded along with their cyclical characters are reliable, while the dates without their cyclical characters are later insertions. However, though the latter dates might be wrong, the events recorded cannot be entirely baseless.

If this suggestion is accepted, the internal discrepancies over dating would be solved. For the other problems of the preface noted, other explanations easily present themselves. For example, the preface itself did not claim that the original text of the *sūtra* was brought to China by Vajrabodhi himself. It might as easily been brought by others.[41] The *sūtra* was not referred to by the two contemporary cataloguers, since the work was only an unfinished manuscript and it was not kept in the the capital Ch'ang-an, where the catalogue and dictionary were compiled. With regard to the style of the *sūtra* in Chinese, it might have followed the Sanskrit textual style, or perhaps the original Sanskrit text itself was an exegesis to the commentary as has been suggested. Moreover, the Bodhisattva Mañjuśrī is popular in Pure Land and Tantric Buddhism.[42] Therefore, there is no problem about the text having a flavor of Pure Land Buddhism and being considered as a later compilation. As regards to the parallel passages which have been noted, this is a characteristic common to many *sūtras*. All these points tend to show that with regard to the information regarding the life of Hye Ch'o, the preface appears reliable. There are certain confusions, however, and the authorship of the preface remains in doubt.

Unlike his relations with Vajrabodhi, our knowledge of which is entirely dependent upon the preface of this *sūtra,* Hye Ch'o's connection with Amoghavajra is attested by independent primary source material. According to a memorial submitted to the Chinese throne by Hye Ch'o it is known that he was sent to the Chou-chih country and successfully prayed for rain near the Jade-maid pool. This took place in March 774.[43] In this memorial, Hye Ch'o called himself a member of the Royal Religious Establishment.[44]

In his will dated 774 Amoghavajra himself states,

> There are many disciples who learnt Dharma from my platform. Eight of them are well-trained in the five sections of canons. After losing some through death, only six are still living. They are Han-kuang of the Chin-ko monastery, Hye Ch'o of Silla... If the young scholars (in future) face any difficulty, you (six disciples) should explain the problems to them. Let not the light of Dharma go out.[45]

Immediately after the death of Amoghavajra, Hye Ch'o and his colleagues sent a memorial to the throne. In that memorial, they gave thanks for royal sympathy bestowed by His Majesty during the funeral of their teacher. They also prayed to maintain the religious establishment founded by their late teacher.[46]

It appears that Hye Ch'o stayed a few more years at Ch'ang-an. According to the preface, during the year 780, he went to the Wu-t'ai Mountain with the incomplete translation of the *sūtra*. He resided at the Ch'ien yuan-p'u-t'i Monastery and there copied the text of the *sūtra* in Chinese.

One would like to know the reason for Hye Ch'o's departure to the Wu-t'ai Mountain. Presumably, he went there on a pilgrimage and for permanent retirement, as he was about eighty years old at the time. Amoghavajra had himself a very close association with the Wu-t'ai Mountain. It was at his initiative that the Chin-ko and Yu-hua monasteries were built and monks attached to these monasteries ordained. Certain other religious establishments were also erected under Amoghavajra's influence.[47] Among Amoghavajra's eminent disciples, Han-kuang resided in, and was possibly the abbot of, Chin-ko Monastery. Amoghavajra's other disciples, Hui-hsiao and Hui-lang were sent to the Wu-t'ai Mountain on different occasions in connection with Royal Religious Services.[48] According to a stone inscription of Amoghavajra written by Yen Cheng, dated 781, only the name of the monk Hui-lang is mentioned as the successor of Amoghavajra.[49] This indirectly proves that after 780. Hye Ch'o was no longer staying at Ch'ang-an. The death of Hye Ch'o, if not proved by his name not being mentioned in this inscription, must have, in any case, occurred soon after.

During his lifetime Hye Ch'o was associated with the introduction of Tantric Buddhism to China.[50] The beginnings of Tantra in China are associated with the Indian master Śubhakarasiṃha who arrived in China in 716, settled at Ch'ang-an and died in 735 at the age of ninety-nine. Hye Ch'o's association with Śubhakarasiṃha is not alluded to in our sources, but that Hye Ch'o at least knew of him seems likely. Hye Ch'o's association with the other two masters of Tantra in China, Vajrabodhi and Amoghavajra, has been previously detailed. Tantra in China was a phenomenon mainly confined to the eight and early ninth centuries. It is interesting to examine the the life of Hye Ch'o in relation to the period of fluoresence of Tantra in China. His life spans the period of the great Tantra masters in China, he appears to have worked closely with at least Vajrabodhi and Amoghavajra (and indirectly, Śubhakarasiṃha) at the centre of Tantra in China, Ch'ang-an. Hye Ch'o was an obscure monk, scarcely of any importance except for the *Memoir* he has left us. It is interesting to speculate that his voyage to India was inspired by Vajrabodhi and perhaps Śubhakarasiṃha in order to gain a better knowledge of Tantra, a form of Buddhism that was at this time beginning to become of some importance in India. Hye Ch'o does not himself allude to his association with the Tantra masters in China. Yet, his biography is in many ways a history of the most important period of Tantra in China.

At present, the text of Hye Ch'o's *Memoir of a Pilgrimage to the Five Regions of India* (*Hui-ch'ao Wang-wu-t'ien-chu-kuo Chuan*) is available only in a fragmentary form. The fragment was recovered from Tun-huang by Paul Pelliot in 1908. The sections of the *Memoir* concerned with Hye Ch'o's outgoing journey and the conclusion of his travels are damaged. Even the extant text is in a condensed form.[51] The content is not so detailed and precise as the memoirs written by Hsüan-tsang and I- ching. Though the calligraphy of the fragment is quite handsome, the text contains many strange characters which are only found in Tun-huang manuscripts and most of which are not even referred to in dictionaries.[52] The structure of sentences is imperfect and it is very diffictult to understand the text clearly.[53]

Literally, Hye Ch'o's style of Chinese prose only attained an average standard. His phrasing and wording, as found in the extant text, are definitely not elegant or masterly. If one compares his writing with those of Hsüan-tsang and his disciples like K'uei-chi and Tao-hsüan,[54] or the pilgrim monk I-ching, there is a clear gap between their literary attainments. There are passages in his *Memoir* which are very vague.[55] Hye Ch'o's poetry, though better than his prose, is still far inferior to that of his Chinese brethren.[56]

Hye Ch'o's knowledge of Indian and Central Asian languages was even poorer. Although he recorded in his *Memoir* the difference in languages between countries, he did not mention any specific names of Indian languages or their dialects. His lack of linguistic training was possibly the reason why proper names are omitted in his *Memoir*. This was perhaps also the reason why he did not become a prominent assistant to the two eminent translators Vajrabodhi and Amoghavajra. Even if we assume that the *sūtra* which we have discussed above was translated or partly translated by him, it is likely that the work was not finished during his lifetime.[57]

In this connection, bibliographical evidence relating to the *Memoir* is signifigant. Yüan-chao, an eminent bibliographer and colleague of of Hye Ch'o did not record the *Memoir* in his catalogue.[58] The possible reason for this omission is that Yüan-chao did not think the memoir achieved an acceptable literary standard. In the *Dictionary,* compiled by Hui-lin, however, the *Memoir* was carefully noted along with other records of travels by Fa-hsien, Hsüan-tsang, etc. As Hui-lin was a native of

Kashgar in Central Asia his appreciation of the *Memoir* was not colored by the conservative Han literary attitude of Yüan-chao. Hui-lin perhaps had a deeper understanding of the *Memoir's* historical value.

Despite the shortcomings of our extant manuscript, Hye-Ch'o's *Memoir* is definitely an important source for Indian and Central Asian history of the early eighth century A. D. The *Memoir* requires a detailed analysis in relation to known historical facts to properly assess that new information Hye Ch'o adds to our knowledge of what is an important, but obscure, period of Indian and Central Asian history. As with other Chinese Buddhist pilgrims, Hye Ch'o recorded facts together with legend. There are certain obvious historiographical weaknesses in the *Memoir*. Hye Ch'o, for example, records many different regions and kingdoms; however most of them receive only brief sketches. The principal cities or capitals of many kingdoms are not named. Hye Ch'o refers to the kings of various kingdoms, but often does not give personal names or titles.

The *Memoir* is, however, above all a contemporary record of historical events and social conditions in India and Central Asia. Such documents are always wanting in ancient Indian history and particularly for the period of the early eighth century. As an example of the historical importance of the *Memoir,* Hye Ch'o is a contemporary witness of the Arab invasions of Western India and Central Asia. He states that when he was in India, the (Tajjikas) or Arabs had overrun one-half of the countries of Western India. The Arabs early invasion of Sindh is well known from Muslim historical sources, but their invasion of the Valabhī kingdon of the Gujerat region of Western India is known only from Valabhī inscriptions. It is known that the Arabs' early progress was halted by 736. Hye Ch'o's *Memoir* is an important record of the progress of this early Muslim attempt to conquer India.[59] His account of the political situation and the progress of the Arab invasions into Central Asia is perhaps of even more interest. The *Memoir* records which countries of Central Asia in 727 were under the control of the Arabs, Turks, Tibetans, Chinese and which were independent. At this period, T'ang China and their Turkish allies were standing in direct confrontation with the Arab military progress into Central Asia. The situation which Hye Ch'o witnessed would not last long, for Chinese control of Central Asia waned after the significant battle of the Talas River in 751, where the Arabs joined with China's former allies, the Turks, to defeat the Korean-Chinese viceroy, Ko Sŏn-ji. Hye Ch'o's memoir is perhaps the last non-Muslim contemporary account of Central Asia before its conquest by the Arabs and Muslim civilization. Central Asia had always been an important area of Buddhist culture, particularly important in the transmission of Buddhism to China. Shortly after Hye Ch'o's visit, Buddhism would disappear from Central Asia and the traditional land route for Buddhist ideas and pilgrims would be blocked by the new, rising cultural force in Asia.

Importance of the Pilgrims' Records

It is perhaps paradoxical that one of the main areas of importance of these records for the modern reader is also the cause of the weakness of the records in other areas. Whatever information the records may or may not contain, they were written for and by Buddhists. Thus, the records are of extreme interest for the student of ancient Indian Buddhist thought and history. All the records contain much interesting and useful historical, political, social and archaeological data in lesser or greater degress, but this must be said to be, in the main, incidental. I- ching, for example, gives little information about the India of his time, beyond the formal activities of Buddhism. Hsüan-tsang, however, relates much information, but his purpose was also primarily concerned with Buddhism; he was giving a tour of Buddhist countries. Although I have previously mentioned the wealth of political information Hye Ch'o gives, he primarily dwells on Buddhist countries. In this connection Thomas Watters has criticized Hsüan-tsang correctly from the viewpoint of the modern historian when he says that,

> His (Hsüan-tsang's) faith was simple and almost unquestioning, and he had an aptitude for belief which has been called credulity. But his was not that credulity which lightly believes the impossible and accepts any statement merely because it is on record and suits the convictions or prejudices of the individual. Hsüan-tsang always wanted to have his own personal testimony, the witness of his own senses or at least his personal experience. It is true his faith helped his unbelief, and it was too easy to convince him where a Buddhist miracle was concerned... But partly because our pilgrim was thus too ready to believe, though partly also for other reasons, he did not make the best use of his opportunities. He was not a good observer, a careful investigator, or a satisfactory recorder, and consequently he left very much untold which he would have done well to.[60]

This criticism of Hsüan-tsang can well be applied to all the pilgrims' records. But Watters also pointedly reminds us that,

> We must remember, however, that Hsüan-tsang in his travels cared little for other things and wanted to know only Buddha and Buddhism. His perfect faith in these, his devotion to them and his enthusiasm for them were remarkable to his contemporaries, but to us they are still more extraordinary.[61]

For the student of ancient Indian Buddhist thought and history the records give an unparalleled account of Buddhist India through the first millennium A. D. I- ching, for example, gives a detailed interpretation of the divisions of Buddhist sects along with their general geographical locations. Hsüan-tsang is also careful to give a detailed geographical account of these sects including the numbers of monks and monasteries at the locations he visited. He also records whether the monks belonged to the Hinayana or Mahayana persuasions. Hsüan-tsang indicates whether the king was friendly or unfriendly towards Buddhism, and the state of health of Buddhism in a particular kingdom.

With reference to the Buddhist scholastic tradition, both I-ching and Hsüan-tsang give useful information. I-ching mentions the great historical masters such as Asaṅga, Vasubandhu, Aśvaghoṣa and Nāgārjuna. He also mentions near contemporaries such as Dharmapāla, as well as logicians, grammarians and his contemporary teachers. Because we know I-ching's dates, we can from his information deduce the approximate dates of the great Buddhist masters, information which is unavailable from Indian sources. I-ching also contributed to our knowledge of Nāgārjuna. He translated what is said to be a private letter to a Sātavāhana king of Western India who dates to *circa* 100 A. D. Both Hsüan-tsang and Hye Ch'o also record traditions concerning Nāgārjuna. From Hsüan-tsang, particularly in the companion volume, the *Life of Hsüan Tsang* by Hui-li, we can obtain a clear picture of the university monastery of Nālanda and of Hsüan-tsang's teacher, the Yogācāra master, Dharmapāla.

The pilgrims also give an excellent impression of popular Buddhist worship and belief. I-ching relates the orthodox tradition of worship and ritual as he understood it. Fa-hsien records actual ceremonies. Hsüan-tsang records the stories and traditions of Buddhism that circulated throughout India. The very credulity of faith which Watters criticizes helps to create the atmosphere in which Buddhism existed at the time. Most importantly, these records are personal narratives of a religion in which the writers deeply believed, a type of record unavailable in the Indian tradition.

If the pilgrims' records are not in all cases perfect historical records, comparable to the Chinese dynastic annals, they are none the less invaluable for the study of ancient Indian history. If India had had a great historical tradition of its own, these records would be, at the most, supplemental source material. However, historical writing was never well developed in India. Thus, classical European and Chinese sources, and such disciplines as epigraphy and numismatics become the main sources of ancient Indian history. Without the personal narratives of the Buddhist pilgrims, our knowledge of ancient Indian history would lack both precise data and personal feeling. The three main areas in which the modern historian is particularly interested are political, social and archaeological. The pilgrims often recorded details of the political developments of an area through which they passed. Sometimes, as in the case of Hye Ch'o these details are explicit as to contemporary political developments. The previously mentioned Arab invasion of India indicated by Hye Ch'o is a good example of the concrete political data which can be obtained from the records. In other cases, exact political details are often incidental to a pilgrim's account. However, with cross reference to other sources and by comparing the accounts of the pilgrims, a connected political picture of an area can be obtained. The area of Northwest India and Central Asia, for example, was visited by all the pilgrims except I-ching. Northwest India and Central Asia have always been an area of much political and cultural intercourse. Fa-hsien visited this area at the time the Kushan empire was in disintegration, just anterior to the rise of the Guptas and the influence they exerted over this area. Fa-hsien gives little exact political data; however, he does recite legends of Kaniṣka he heard while in Gandhāra. Kaniṣka had been the last great king to rule over this area before Fa-hsien's arrival. The pilgrim Sung Yün, whose travels were confined to Northwest India, describes an extremely interesting period of its political history. Sung Yün arrived in a period of political confusion. Nomadic peoples known as the White Huns, or Ephthalites, had invaded this area. These invasions had a deleterious effect on the state of Buddhism and were the cause of Sung Yün not being able to proceed to India proper. In fact, the main interest of the modern historian in Sung Yün's account is his description of this period of invasions, an obscure period of Indian history. It can be deduced, for example, that the king of Gandhāra whom Sung Yün met was named Mihirakula. At this time, he was occupied with a war with Kaśmīr, and it is probably for this reason that Sung Yün was unable to proceed past Gandhāra. Hsüan-tsang travelled through Northwest India and Central Asia when it was under the control of the Western Turks. He had to obtain a guarantee of safe conduct from the king of the Turks to be able to pass through this area. In Hsüan-tsang's time the great empire of Harṣa was also exerting its influence here. Hsüan-tsang was, in fact, a good friend of the Emperor and the personal account of Harṣa given in Hsüan-tsang's biography is unique in the study of ancient Indian political history. Finally, Hye Ch'o visited the extreme North-west India and Central Asia in a period when a new political and cultural force had arisen, that of the Arabs. Thus taken together, the pilgrims' account can build a composite chronological record of an area. The wealth of political data, both direct and indirect, is invaluable for the historian.

For the modern social historian, the accounts of the pilgrims are of particular interest. All the pilgrims, except I-ching, recorded details of the contemporary Indian society which they saw. As travellers from a foreign land, it is natural that the pilgrims would record strange social customs and traditions. Hsüan-tsang, in particular, was careful to record certain social details of the countries he visited. Invariably, he records the physical details of a country, its size, climate and the crops then grown. He also gives an appraisal of the demeanor of the people. Then, because he was a Buddhist pilgrim, Hsüan-tsang records the religious inclinations of the society he visited. He was, of course, particularly interested in the social position of Buddhism. Hye Ch'o also records social details. His records are perhaps superior to Hsüan-tsang's in this respect, because he records what particularly interests him in a country rather than recording the details in a formulaic style as does Hsüan-tsang. Hye Ch'o also notes the products and agriculture of a country, and peculiarities of dress and appearance of the inhabitants of the countries he visits, as well as of course, the social position of Buddhism. He however, adds other valuable details, such as describing the method of petition to a Central Asian king. Precise and valuable social data with particular reference to Buddhism can be obtained from the pilgrims' records. For example, Hsüan-tsang records the fact that Nālanda was bought for the Buddhist order by merchants for ten *koṭis*. Hsüan-tsang's biography records that Nālanda was supported from the revenues of one-hundred villages. Again, such precise social information is unavailable from contemporary literary sources in the Indian tradition.

For the modern archaeologist and art historian, the records, particularly that of Hsüan-tsang, are an invaluable source. They record the locations of important Buddhist monuments throughout India. In the case of Hsüan-tsang, he details the exact local geographical locations of buildings and monuments he saw. For the archaeologist, this greatly helps the process of identification of sites he excavates. Hsüan-tsang, in fact, can be said to be a guide to the monuments of Buddhist India of his day. His work compares to that of Pausanias, who wrote an ancient guide to the antiquities of Greece. At such sites a Bodhgayā, Rājgir and Nālanda, Hsüan-tsang gives the modern reader a tour of the monuments he saw. General Alexander Cunningham, the great nineteenth-century Indologist was able to locate such important sites as Nālanda and Vaiśāīi by merely following the directions given by Hsüan-tsang. When these sites were later excavated some attempt could be made to identify the buildings found only because of the information supplied by Hsüan-tsang.

Reasons for Retranslation of These Records

Fifty years ago, the great historian of ancient India, Vincent Smith, said of Fa-hsien's records,

> The final translation of Fa-hsien's *Travels,* equipped with an up-to-date commentary adequately fulfilling the requirements of both Chinese and Indian scholarship, has not yet appeared; and the production of such a work by a single writer is almost impossible.[62]

This comment, which can be equally applied to all the pilgrims' records, is certainly even more true today. The translations which exist today are the products of nineteenth-century scholarship, as can be seen from the attached bibliography. While these translations were adequate or good for their time, major advances have since been made in both Chinese and Indian scholarship. In one case, that of Hye Ch'o, an English translation and commentary has never been published. Because of the importance of these for Indian history and culture, now is the time for a major retranslation project to be undertaken.

The first area in which many advances have been made in scholarship is linguistic. The records themselves are, of course, written in Chinese. Translation of ancient Chinese manuscript has advanced in both the understanding of meanings and in style.

While the records were written in Chinese, they deal with India, thus a thorough knowledge of Indian languages is essential. The pilgrims undertook to make Indian proper names, places and Buddhist technical terminology understandable to their Chinese audience. Thus, one of the main tasks of the modern translator is the reconstruction of such proper names and places back into their original Indian form. This branch of scholarship, which is consistent with the cross-cultural nature of the records, was little understood when the records were first translated. The pilgrims themselves recognized the difficulty of construing Indian words into Chinese. I-ching devotes a chapter to Sanskrit grammar and poetics. The work which has been done in this century in Chinese translations of Buddhist works, can now be utilized to arrive at an accurate translation of the often used proper names, places and Buddhist technical terms.

The advances made in the history and archaeology of ancient India have made it possible to fully utilize the advances that have been made in linguistics. It is now possible to identify the sites and personages mentioned by the pilgrims with greater accuracy than was before possible. As mentioned above, General Cunningham used Hsüan-tsang to discover and identify important archaeological sites. These sites have since been excavated. The modern scholar is able to use the data from these excavations to make a more precise translation of the pilgrims' records. In major sites such as Sārnāth, Bodhgayā, Nālanda and Rājgir, described by many pilgrims, we can use the records to identify the precise location and function of individual buildings and monuments. This type of archaeological evidence was not available to the early translators of these records.

Details of ancient Indian history have become much more clear since the records were first translated. Through the discoveries made in numerous archaeological sites, the advances made in the fields of epigraphy, numismatics and textual criticism, much more of what pilgrims mention can be understood in relation to the newly-developed historical framework of ancient India. Historians have carefully studied the relevant historical information contained in the records since they have become well known. The modern translator thus has a superior grasp of ancient Indian history and is better able to translate and comment upon historical references. It is to be hoped that new translations will cause other scholars to elucidate further new historical information from the records. In the case of Hye Ch'o a new tanslation is of particular value for historians who do not read Chinese or have access to the little known German translation.

Many scholars of ancient India, as could be expected from their subject matter, do not have the ability to read Chinese. Because of the importance of these records to many branches of ancient Indian scholarship, an accurate series of translations is now essential. A series of translations which is standard in transliteration, rendered in a modern reading style, and which incorporates the latest advances in scholarship is much needed. A new series of translations is needed to commemorate one of the greatest stories of contact between two great cultures in the name of religion. The importance and uniqueness of this contact to a modern audience can best be seen by an incident Fa-hsien records;

> When Fa-hsien and Tao-ching first arrived at the Jetavana monastery, and thought how the World-honoured one had formerly resided there for twenty-five years, painful reflections arose in their minds. Born in a border-land, along with their like-minded friends, they had travelled through so many kingdoms; some of those friends had

returned (to their own land), and some had (died), proving the impermanence and uncertainty of life; and to-day they saw the place where Buddha had lived now unoccupied by him. They were melancholy through their pain of heart, and the crowd of monks came out, and asked them from what kingdom they were come. 'We are come,' they replied, 'from the land of Han.' 'Strange,' said the monks with a sigh, 'that men of a border country should be able to come here in search of our Law!' Then they said to one another, 'During all the time that we, preceptors and monks, have succeeded to one another, we have never seen men of Han, followers of our system, arrive here.'[63]

Thus began this unique period of contact between the Indian and Chinese cultures.

Bibliography

Fa-hsien

S. Beal. *Travels of Fa Hian and Sung yün.* London, 1869.
revised in *Buddhist Records of the Western World.* London, 1884.

H. A. Giles. *The Travels of Fa-Hsien* (399–414) *or Record of Buddhistic. Kingdoms.* Shanghai and London, 1877. Cambridge, 1923

James Legge. *A Record of Buddhistic Kingdoms.* Oxford, 1886.

M. Abel Rémusat. *Revu, Completé, et Augmenté d'Eclaircissements Nouveaux par M. M. Klaproth et Landresse.* Paris, 1836.

Sung yün

S. Beal. *Travels of Fa Hian and Sung yün.* London, 1869. retranslated in *Buddhist Records of the Western World.* London, 1884.

Edouard Chavannes. *Voyage de Sung-yün dans l'Udyana et le Gandhara.* Hanoi, 1903.

Hsüan-tsang

S. Beal. *Buddhistic Records of the Western World.* London, 1884. *Life of Hiuen Tsiang by the Shamans Hwui Li and Yen Tsung.* London, 1888, 1911.

I-ching

J. Takakusu. *A Record of The Buddhist Religion.* Oxford, 1896.

Notes

1 James Legge, *A Record of Buddhistic Kingdoms* (Oxford, 1886), pp. 9–10.

2 Legge, *op. cit.*, p. 12.

3 Legge, *op. cit.*, pp. 115–116.

4 Samuel Beal, *Si-Yu-Ki, Buddhist Records of the Western World* (London, 1884), p. xciv.

5 Beal, *op. cit.*, p. c.

6 Samuel Beal, *The Life of Hiuen-Tsiang* (London, 1911), pp. 2–3.

7 Beal, *op. cit.*, p. 3.

8 Beal, *op. cit.*, p. 10.

9 Beal, *Si-Yu-Ki, op. cit.*, p. 15.

10 Beal, *op. cit.*, p. 16.

11 Beal, *op. cit.*, p. 6.

12 J. Takakusu, *A Record of the Buddhist Religion* (Oxford, 1896), p. 204.

13 Takakusu, *op. cit.*, p. 18.

14 This introduction to Hye Ch'o is an adaptation and expansion of "Hui-ch'ao and his Works: A Reassessment," by Jan Yün-hua, *Indo-Asian Culture,* XII, 3, 1964, pp. 177–190, with additional details supplied by Han Sung yang and myself. (LP)

15 Pelliot, Paul, "Un bibliothèque médiéval retrouvée," *B. E. F. E. O.*, VIII (1908), pp. 511–512 for details. (LP)

16 Full bibliographical details prior to 1938 can be found in the initial translation of Hye Ch'o by W. Fuchs, "Huei-ch'ao's Pigerreise dürch Nordwest-Indian und Zentral-Asien um 726," *Sonderausgabe ausden Sitzunsberichten der Preubischen Akademie der Wissenschaften Phil.-hist. Klasse* XXX (1938). See attached bibliography.

17 In one of his poems, Hye Ch'o wrote: "My country is in the north horizon." This indicated the general direction of his homeland. In the text of the last will and testament of Amoghavajra, Hye Ch'o was clearly mentioned as Hye Ch'o of Hsin-lo. Cf. *Taishō Shinshū Daizōkyō* (*Taishō edition of the Tripiṭaka in Chinese,* hereafter referred to as T.) vols. LIV, 926 LII, 844b.

18 cf. p. 14.

19 Cf. *Mikkyō Daijiten* (*A Encyclopedia of Tantric Buddhism)* ed. by Mistunaga Shodo (Kyoto, 1931–33), p. 152b and J. Takakusu, *E cho den Kō* (*A Biographical study on Hui-ch'ao)* in *Dai Nihon Bukkyō Zensho* (*The Complete Collection of Buddhist Books in Japanese)* ed. Toyohachi, 1910–11 1931, note 1.

20 For problems of Hye Ch'o's relation with Vajrabodhi, cf. p.15 ff.

21 Han Sung yang relates the account of the childhood of a monk from

Korea called Hye T'ong found in the *Milgyo Puljŏn* (*Ch'ongji Pŏpchang*). The account is interesting in that it appears Hye T'ong's life was in many ways parallel to Hye ch'o's. It is said that,

> In his childhood one day he was playing on the Tongge river and happened to catch a wild sow. Killing the wild sow and skinning it, he left the bones in the back garden. Next morning when he went to see the bones again, these bones had disappeared. However, because there was a trace of blood, he followed it, then he reached the den of the wild sow. When he entered there, he saw the same wild sow hugging five small young. At this time he was very much moved at this scene of the wild sow being alive, and because of this strange phenomenon, he got an inspiration to become a Buddhist monk. After this incident, in order to study Buddhism more deeply he went to T'ang China, where he met his Indian teacher Śubhakarasiṃha .... discussion of For Śubhakarasiṃha, cf. p. (LP)

cf. Yün-hua, Jan, "Some new Light on Kuśinagara from The Memoir of Hui-ch'ao," *Oriens Extremus,* XII, 1, 1965, p. 58, note 12. (LP)

23 These names are given in Hui-lin's quotations, T. LIV, 926c. For identifications of these names, see P. Pelliot, "Deux itineraires de Chine en Inde," *B. E. F. E. O.* IV (1904) and Takakusu's translation of I-ching's record. See also a recent study by Hsü Yun-chiao, *Nan-yang Shih* (*A History of the South Sea)* Singapore, 1961.

24 Cf. T. LIV. 927b.

25 Cf. Yun-hua, Jan, "South India in the VIII Century Hui-ch'ao's description re-examined," *Oriens Extremus,* XII, 1, 1968, pp. 169–177. (LP)

26 Cf. Yün-hua, Jan, "West India According to Hui-ch'ao's Record," *Indian Historical Quarterly,* vol. 39, nos. 1&2, 1963, pp. 27–37. (LP)

27 Cf. Fuchs, *op. cit.,* p. 427.

28 Usually, the term *pei-shu* has been translated as "copyist" or "scribe", one who records Sanskrit dictations made by the chief translator. But in many cases, the main duty of translating actually fell to the *pei-shu,* especially when the chief translator's knowledge of Chinese was not strong.

29 Original text of this preface and the translation exists in T. XX, 724–775c. (No. 1177a & Nanjio No. 1044).

30 Cf. Mochizuki Shinkō, *Bukkyō Daijiten* (*An Encyclopedia of Buddhism),* Kyoto, 1931–36, p. 2386b. and Kanbayashi Ryjyo's contribution to *Bussho Kaisetsu Daijiten* (*A Bibliographical Dictionary of Buddhist Books),* ed. Ono Genmyo, Tokyo, 1936, vol. VII, p. 354b–357b.

31 Cf. Chou Yi-liang, "Tantricism in China," *H. J. A. S.* VIII (1945), p. 282, note 56.

32 *Ibid.* p. 299ff.

33 T. 2157, vol, LV, fascicles xv-xvi and T. 2128, vol. LIV, 926.

34 Cf. Nai-yin's *Liang-pu-ta-fa Hsiang-ch'eng-shih-tzu fu-fa Chi* (*A Record on the Succession-line of the Mastership of the Two Sects),* T. LI, 784c.

35 I. e., the second year of the Sheng-yuan age of the South T'ang Kingdom; see T. LV, 1084b.

36 Cf. Mochizuki Shinkō, *Bukkyō Kyōten Seiritsu Shi Ron* (*Historical Studies on the formation of Buddhist canons)*, Kyoto, 1946, p. 519–31.

37 Cf. note no. 19.

38 Besides the evidence cited below, there must be certain reasons for the preface to allege the name of Hye Ch'o as a *pei-shu,* otherwise why from amongst the many eminent monks of the sect, should the author of the preface choose this Korean monk as the *pei-shu?*

39 T. XX, 724, preface line 1.

40 *Ibid.* line 6.

40a For example, Ch'en Yin-k'o has remarked that to identify the cyclical characters, the title of reign, and the acutal date is a very difficult task. Even an eminent historian like Tao-hsüan made similar mistakes. Cf. *Nan-yüeh-ta-shih Li-shih-yüan-wen pa* (*Notes on the Autobiography of Hui-ssü) Bulletin of the Institute of History and Philosophy, Academia Sinica,* vol. III (1932), p. 300ff.

41 After Vajrabodhi's arrival in China, there were other persons who went to China from India. For instance, Hye Ch'o himself came back to China in 727. Mitra, a monk from North India, went to China in 729.

42 Cf. *Mikkyō Daijiten,* p. 2167–69. For Amoghavajra's translations of canons concerning Mañjuśrī cf. *Shōwa hōbō sōmokuoku,* vol. I, p. 683b, 684a-c. About Amoghavajra's effort for the establishment of Mañjuśrī worship see note 47 below.

43 The original text of this memorial is in T. LII, 843b & 855a.

44 Hye Ch'o addressed himself as a Śramana of *Nei-tao-ch'ang,* or Royal Religious Establishment, in the memorial written by him.

45 The original text is in T. LII, 844a & b.

46 In the original text of this memorial, as well as in the text of Amoghavajra'a last will and textament, Hye Ch'o was ranked second among the names of the the disciples of Amoghavajra. *Ibid.* 845b.

47 On the names and dates of temples of Mañjuśrī constructed by Amoghavajra, see *Ibid.* 834a–835c, 837a, 840c, 841c . . .

48 *Ibid.* 858b-859b.

47 *Ibid.* 860b line 20.

50 Cf. K. Ch'en *Buddhism in China.* (Princeton, 1964), pp. 325–337; Chou Yi-liang, *op. cit.;* J. Takakusu, *The Essentials of Buddhist Philosophy* (Honolulu, 1947), pp. 144–147. (LP)

51 Lo Chen-yu has rightly pointed out that according to Hui-lin's *Dictionary,* the division of Hye Ch'o's *Memoir* was in three fascicles. But the fragment that was recovered from Tun-huang is without any division of fascicle. Moreover, there are a few quotations which are preserved in Hui-lin's *Dictionary* but not in the fragment. This proves that the fragment is a condensed

version of the *Memoir*. Cf. *Hsüeh-t'ang chiao-k'an ch'un-shu hsü-lu* (*Introductory notes to the books published by Lo Chen-yu*, Peking, 1909), fasc. II, pp. 35–36.

52 Cf. Lo's textual reading and W. Fuchs' translation of the *Memoir*. About the strange and variant writing of Chinese characters as found in the Tun-huang Mss., see Chiang Hung-li, *Tun-huang pien-wen tzu-yi t'ung shih* (*Word and Phrases in "Pien-wen" recovered from Tun-huang*), Peking, 2nd and Enlarged ed., 1961.

53 There are quite a good number of such examples in the text of the *Memoir;* see Ch'ien Tao-sun's edition, p. 3b, 11a, 25a, 27b . . .

54 Hsüan-tsang and Pien-chi's *Hsi-yū chi,* I-ching's records and Tao-hsüan's historical works are all written in a very high standard of Chinese prose. Their styles, phrasing, etc. are all elegant and beautiful, their works are definitely far superior to those of the *Memoir* by Hye Ch'o.

55 cf. Yün-hua, Jan, "Hui-ch'ao's record on Kashmir," *Kashmir Research Biannual,* II (1961), pp. 115–124.

56 For instance the poems of Han-shan, see Wu Ch'i-yu, "A Study of Han-shan," *T'oung-pao* XLV (1957), p. 411.

57 Even the preface stated that Hye Ch'o studied the *sūtra* under Vajrabodhi for eight years, but was still unable to finish the work.

58 See note 33.

59 Cf. R. C. Majumdar, ed. *History and Culture of the Indian People,* vol. III, *The Classical Age,* p. 558.

60 Thomas Watters, *On Yuan Chwang's Travels in India* (London, 1904–05), pp. 14–15.

61 Watters, *op. cit.,* p. 15.

62 Vincent A. Smith, *The Early History of India* (Oxford, 1924), p. 25.

63 James Legge, *A Record of Buddhistic Kingdoms* (Oxford, 1886), pp. 57–58.

Part II

Translation of *Memoir of a Pilgrimage to the Five Regions of India*

1. Vaiśālī (?)

[... they do not honor the Three] Jewels ...[1] They go barefoot and naked. The non-believers do not wear clothes ...[2] They eat at any time because they do not observe *uposatha.* The land is completely flat... They have [no] slaves.[3] The crime of selling people is not different from that of murder ...

2. Kuśinagara

After a month's journey, I arrived at the country of Kuśinagara.[4] This is where the Buddha entered *nirvana.* The city is desolate and no people live there. The *stūpa* was built at the site where the Buddha entered *nirvāṇa.*[5] There is a *dhyāna* master[6] who keeps the place clean. Every year on the eighth day of the eighth month,[7] monks, nuns, clergy and laymen hold a great assembly of worship there. [On this occasion], numerous banners which were seen by all people would appear in the sky. On the same day, many people would resolve their minds [for the religion].

West of the *stūpa* is the Airāvatī river.[8] The river flows two thousand *li* southwards before it enters the Ganges.[9] The *stūpa* is isolated on all sides; no people go there. The forests are very deserted. Those on pilgrimage are [often] wounded by rhinoceros and tigers.[10]

Thirty *li* southeast from the *stūpa* is a monastery named Bandhana.[11] There are more than thirty villages [allocated to this monastery, three or four of which][12] constantly make offerings to the *dhyāna* masters to enable them to maintain religious services at the *stūpa* ...

3. Vārānasī

[After ...] days I arrived at the country of Vārānasī.[13] This country is also desolate. There is no king ...

... the band of five [headed by Kauṇḍinya].[14] I saw a clay statue on the *stūpa.*[15]

On top [of the pillar] there is a [statue of] a lion. The pillar is extremely beautiful.[16] [Its circumference measures that of] five people[17] with joined arms. The lines carved on it are delicate. The pillar was made at the time the *stūpa* [was constructed]. The monastery is named the Dharmacakra Sanghārāma . . .[18]

The non-believers wear no clothes. They smear ashes on their bodies[19] and worship Mahādeva.[20] In this monastery there are gilt bronze images [of the Buddha] and the five hundred [Pratyeka Buddhas].[21] These images were made by Śīlāditya,[22] a former king of Magadha.[23] He also made a gilt [*dharma* wheel], which is over thirty paces in diameter.[24] The city is built on the northern bank of the Ganges.

This Deer Park, along with Kuśinagara, Rajagṛha and Mahābodhi are the four great holy *stūpas*.[25] All these are situated in the territory of the Magadha kingdom. Both Mahāyāna and Hīnayāna are practised in this country.

. . .[26] I arrived at the Mahābodhi monastery. I was very happy as my long cherished wish had been fulfilled. I expressed my humble wishes in a five-word poem:

Untroubled by the distance to Mahābodhi
Unafraid that the Deer Park is far,
Only the dangerous path worried me.
Not caring how the evil wind blows.
To visit the eight *stūpas*[27] is truly not easy.[28]
All places[29] were burnt.[30]
How then could one's desire be fulfilled?[31]
With my eyes I saw it this very day.

4. Central India and the Customs of the Five Regions of India

From the country of Vārānasī [I walked west for a] month and arrived at the city where the central-Indian king resides. The place is called Kānyakubja.[32] The territory of the central-Indian king is very broad and the inhabitants are many.[33] The king possesses nine hundred elephants while other great chiefs possess two to three hundred each. The king himself often leads troops into battle and frequently fights with the other four regions of India. The central-Indian king is always victorious.[34] According to the conventions of the countries, when one knows that it possesses a smaller number of elephants and soldiers, it immediately begs for peace and pays tribute annually. They do not fight on the battlefield and kill each other.

The dress, language, customs, and laws of the five regions of India are similar. Only the language of the village folk in south India is different.[35] The class of officials is not different from that of central India.

The national laws of the five regions of India prescribe no cangue, beatings or prison. Those who are guilty are fined in accordance with the degree of the offence committed. There is no capital punishment.[36] From the king down to the common people one sees no pleasure hunting with falcons or dogs or such similar activities. Although there are many bandits on the roads, they let their victims go alive[37] after taking away their things. If the victim holds his things too dear, then he will at once suffer for it.[38]

The land is very warm. All plants are always green. There is no frost or snow. The foods include rice, baked wheat flour,[39] butter, milk and curds.[40] Soy is not available but salt is. Everybody eats food cooked in earthenware pots. They do not have iron cauldrons or similar things.

Apart from paying one *picul* of grain out of every five to the king annually, the people have no other labor service or taxes. The king sends his own men to transport [the grain]; it is not the duty of the landowners. Most people of the land are poor; few are rich. Those from the royal family, official households, and the rich wear a pair of cotton cloths. Ordinary people wear one piece while the poor wear only half a piece. Women do the same.

Whenever the king sits in audience, chiefs and commoners all come and sit around him. Everyone argues for his own cause. Charges and countercharges are many and it becomes very confusing and noisy. The king listens but does not become angry. Deliberating, he passes judgement saying, 'you are right' or 'you are wrong'. The commoners and others take the word of the king as final and complain no further.

The king and the chiefs sincerely honor and worship the Three Jewels. If they meet a monk-master, they sit on the ground, unwilling to sit on couches. The king and chiefs take their couches with them wherever they go or stay. They rest on them wherever they are and never use the couches of others. Monasteries and royal houses are all three-storeyed buildings. The ground floors are used as storage rooms while the upper floors are for dwelling. The [houses of the] great chiefs are the same. These houses are all even roofed, made of bricks and wood. Other houses are straw huts similar to the gabled Chinese house.[41] They are also one-storeyed.

The products of the land are only cotton cloth, elephants, horses, and other things. The land itself does not produce gold and silver, which are imported from foreign countries. Domestic animals such as camels, mules, asses, and pigs are not kept. Most cows are white. Among ten thousand head there is rarely one which is red or black. Both sheep and horses are few. Only the king has two to three hundred sheep and sixty to seventy horses. The great chiefs and the common people do not keep these domestic animals. They are only interested in rearing cattle, as they obtain milk, curds, and butter from them. The people of the land are good natured. They do not like killing. In the markets one does not see any butchering or meat selling.

5. The Four Great *Stūpas* of Central India

Both Māhāyana and Hīnayāna are practised in central India. In the territory of central India there are four great *stūpas*. Three are situated north of the Ganges. One is located at the Anāthapiṇḍika[42] park in Śrāvastī.[43] There are monasteries and monks there. The second one is at the Amarāpalī[44] park in Vaiśālī. The *stūpa* still exists but the monastery is deserted and ruined and without monks. The third one is situated in Kapilavastu[45], the city where the Buddha was born. The Aśoka tree is still there but the city is already ruined. There is a *stūpa* but no monks or inhabitants. The city is situated at the northernmost part [of the country].[46] The forests are mostly deserted and there are many bandits on the roads. It is very difficult for those on pilgrimage to go safely.

The fourth [great *stūpa*] is the *stūpa* with the three-laned jeweled staircase[47] situated at a distance of seven days' journey west of the city where the central-Indian king resides. It lies between two streams of the Ganges. This is the place where the Buddha descended from the *Trāyastrimśa*[48] heaven to *Jambudvīpa*[49] by magically creating a three-laned jeweled staircase. The left lane is golden, the right one is silver, and the middle one is glazed with *vaiḍūrya*. The Buddha came down the middle lane, Brahma[50] from the left lane, Śākra[51] from the right lane, both attending the Buddha. At this very spot a *stūpa* was constructed. At present, there are monasteries and monks.[52]

6. South India

From central India, walking south for more than three months, I arrived at the place[53] where the south Indian king[54] resides. The king has eight hundred elephants. His territory is very broad: the south extends to the Southern sea, the east to the Eastern sea, the west to the Western sea, and the north adjoins the borders of central, west and east India. The dress, food, and customs are similar to those of central India. Only the languages are slightly different. The land is hotter than central India. The products of this land are cotton cloth, elephants, water buffalo, and yellow cattle. Also, there are fewer sheep. They do not have camels, mules and asses. They have rice fields but no sorghum or millet. As for things such as floss and thin silks, they are not available in the five regions of India.

The king, the chiefs[55], and the common people highly revere the Three Jewels. There are many monasteries and monks. Both Mahāyāna and Hīnayāna are practised. In the mountains there is a large monastery which was constructed[56] by *Yakṣas*[57] under order from the *Bodhisattva* Nāgārjuna[58] and not built by human beings. Moreover, the pillars were cut from [rocks of the] mountain and built in three storys. The monastery is over three hundred paces in circumference. During the days when Nāgārjuna was alive, the monastery had three thousand monks. Only fifteen *piculs* of rice[59] were given daily to them for maintenance, but the rice was never exhausted. [The excess rice] would be returned immediately, but afterwards there would be no reduction [in the supply]. But at present the monastery is ruined and there are no monks. Seven hundred years after Nāgārjuna this place began to decay.

When I was on the way to south India, I composed a poem in the five-word style:

On a moonlit night I looked towards the homeward path,[60]
Floating clouds return by the wind.
I wish this letter to go with this opportunity,
The wind blows too fast; the clouds neither listen or return.
My country is in the northern horizon,
Other lands lie at the western extremity.
No wild geese[61] in the hot south[62],
Who will take my words to the homeland?[63]

7. West India

From south India I walked North for two months and arrived at the city where the king[64] of west India resides. The west Indian king also possesses five to six hundred elephants.[65] The products of this land are cotton cloth, silver, elephants, horses, sheep, and cows. Barley, wheat, and various kinds of beans are produced in large quantities [but the production of] rice and corn is much less. Food is mainly bread, wheat preparations, curds, butter, and ghee. In the markets, silver money and cotton cloth are used.

The king, the chiefs, and the common people highly revere and believe in the Three Jewels. There are many monasteries and monks.

Both Mahāyāna and Hīnayāna are practised.

The land is very broad. To the west it reaches the Western sea. The people of this country are good at singing. [In this] the other four regions of India cannot be compared with this country. Here there is no cangue, beating, prison, capital punishment, and similar affairs. At present half the country has been invaded by the Arabs[66] and is already ravaged. According to the law of the five regions of India, those who travel do not carry food. They can beg for food wherever they go. When the king and the chiefs travel, they take food with them so as not to bother the people.

8. North India (Jālandhara)

For over three months I travelled north from west India and arrived at the country of north India, which is called Jālandhara.[67] The king of this country has three hundred elephants. He resides in a city built on the hillside. From the hills the place gradually stretches northwards. As a country it is very narrow. The army and cavalry are small. It is often annexed by the central Indian king and Kaśmīr.[68] This is the reason [the king] resides on the hillside.

The customs, dress, and language are not different from those of central India. The land is slightly cooler than central India and the other regions. There is also no frost or snow, but there is a cold wind. The products of this land are elephants.[69] cotton cloth, rice, and wheat. Mules and asses are few. The king possesses a hundred horses, while each chief has three to five, and the common people have none. The western part of the country is a plain and the eastern part is close to the snowy mountains. There are many monasteries and monks in this country. Both Mahāyāna and Hīnayāna are practised.

9. Suvarṇagotra

A small kingdom is to the east, a month's journey through the snowy mountains. It is called Suvarṇagotra. and is under the control of the Tibetans.[70] The dress is similar to that of north India, but the language is different. The land is extremely cold.

10. Takka

From Jālandhara I walked west and after a month arrived at the country called Takka.[71] The language is slightly different, but the dress, customs, products of the land, climate, and temperature are similar to north India. There are also many many monasteries and monks. Both Mahāyāna and Hīnayāna are practised. The king, chiefs, and common people greatly revere the Three Jewels.

11. Sindhukula

From Takka I walked towards the west for another month and arrived at the country of Sindhukula.[72] The dress, customs, climate, and temperature are similar to north India, although the language is slightly different. This country has many camels from which the people obtain milk and butter for food. The king and the people greatly revere the Three Jewels. There are many monasteries and monks. Sanghabhadra[73], the Reverend Master of the *Śāstras* and author of the *Nyāyānusāra-śāstra*[74] was a native of this country. Both Mahāyāna and Hīnayāna are practised in this country. At present it is being invaded by the Arabs and half of its territory has been lost. From this land to the five regions of India [people] rarely drink much. I have traveled across the five regions, but have not seen any drunken brawls. Those who drink do so only for the sake of energy and strength[75], but nothing more. I did not see any people who excessively enjoyed dance, drama, and feasting.

12. Tamasavana

Further from north India[76] there is a monastery called Tamasavana.[77] During the days when the Buddha was still alive he came and preached the *dharma* there. He enlightened large numbers of human and divine beings. There is a *stūpa* on the bank of a stream east of the monastery where the hair and nails[78] of the Buddha are preserved. At present, there are over three hundred monks. The monastery also has the relic tooth, bone, and other things of a great Pratyeka Buddha.[79] There are seven or eight other monasteries. Each of these has five to six hundred monks. The monasteries are well-managed.[80] They are highly respected by the king and common people.

13. Nagaradhana

There is another monastery called Nagaradhana situated in the mountains. There was a Chinese monk who died in this monastery. The senior monks[81] of the monastery said that the Chinese monk had come from central India and was brilliant and well-versed in the sacred teachings of the *Tripiṭaka*. He was about to return to his homeland, but suddenly fell ill and immediately died. Upon hearing the story, I grieved deeply. Thus, I wrote a poem in four rhymes to commemorate the monk who is now dead. The poem is in the five-word style:

The lamp at your home village has no owner,
The jewel tree fell in another country.
Where does the spirit go?
The precious countenance[82] has turned into ashes.
Pondering this my sorrow is deep.
I grieve that your wish was not fulfilled.
Who knows the road to his native land?
Nothing to be seen but white clouds returning.

14. Kaśmir

From there [Sindhukula] I walked north for fifteen days, entered a mountainous place, and reached the country of Kaśmīr.[83] Kaśmīr is counted as part of north India. It is a rather big country. The king possesses three hundred elephants and resides in the mountains. The roads are dangerous and bad. It has not been invaded by any foreign country. The population of this country is quite flourishing. The poor are many and the rich are few. The dress of the king, chiefs, and rich men is not different from that of central India. The common people cover[84] their ugly bodies with woolen blankets.

The products of this land are copper, iron, cotton cloth, woolen blankets, cows, and sheep. There are elephants, a few horses[85], rice, grapes,[86] and other things. The land is extremely cold, which is different from the countries mentioned before. There is frost in autumn and snow in winter. In summer there is plenty of rainfall.[87] The plants are always green and the leaves thick. In winter the grasses wither.[88]

The valley is narrow and small. From south to north it takes a journey of five days. From east to west, it takes one day to complete the journey. These are the boundaries of the valley. The rest [of the country] is dense mountains. The roofs of the houses are covered by rows of planks. Straw and tiles are not used. The king, chiefs, and the common people greatly revere the Three Jewels. There is a dragon pool. The dragon king[89] gives daily offerings to one thousand *arhat* monks.[90] Although no one has witnessed these holy monks taking food, after the offerings, cakes and rice have been seen coming up from below the water. From this it is known [that they receive food]. To this day these offerings have not ceased. The king and chiefs ride on elephants when they go out. Minor officials ride on horses while the common people all go on foot. There are numerous monasteries and monks in the country. Both

Mahāyāna and Hīnayāna are practised.

Following the practice of the five regions of India, from the king, the queen, consorts, and princes[91], down to the chiefs and their wives, all separately build monasteries in accordance with their respective capabilities. They say when each person has his own meritorious virtues, why should joint effort be necessary? Such being the case, other princes follow that [practice].

Whenever a monastery is built, a village and its inhabitants are immediately donated as an offering to the Three Jewels. Building a monastery without making any donation of a village and its folk is not done. It being the practice of this foreign country, the king and his wives[92] have separate villages with their inhabitants. The princes and chiefs also have their villages and their inhabitants which they donate independently without consulting the king.[93] This also applies in the case of building monasteries. When necessary to build, they do so, and the king is not asked. The king dares not stand in the way because he is afraid that it would taint him with bad deeds.[94]

As for the rich commoners, though having no villages to donate, they also try their best to build monasteries and manage them by themselves. Whenever they obtain things, they offer them to the Three Jewels. As in the five regions of India, human beings are not sold. Since there are no slaves, it is necessary to donate villages and their inhabitants [to the monasteries].

15. Greater Bolor

From Kaśmīr I crossed the mountains and travelled northeast for fifteen days. The countries here are Greater Bolor[95], Yang-t'ung[96], and Sha-po-tz'u.[97] These three countries are all under Tibetan authority. The dress, language, and customs of the people are all different. People wear furs, cotton shirts, boots, and trousers. The land is narrow and the mountains and streams are extremely dangerous. There are also monasteries and monks. People respect and believe in the Three Jewels. Eastwards from here is Tibet [where] there are no monasteries or houses [and where] Buddhism is not known. Because the people [of Greater Bolor, Yang-t'ung and Sha-po-tz'u] are Hu people[98], they believe [in Buddhism].

16. Tibet

To the east lies Tibet. It is situated among glaciers, snowy mountains and valleys. People dwell in tents made of felt. Here there are no cities, suburbs or houses. The residential quarters are similar to those of the Turks.[99] Their dwellings shift with the course of water and grass. Though the king stays in a fixed place, there is no city. He resides and carries on with his work in felt tents. The products of this land include sheep, horses, yaks, and woolens.[100] The dress [of the people] is made of woolens and furs. The dress of the women is the same. The land is extremely cold, unlike the other countries. Usually the food of families is parched grain; rice and pastry are rare.[101] The king and the common people all do not know Buddhism. There are no monasteries or houses.[102] The people hollow[103] out the ground and thus make earthen beds to sleep on. There are no couches and mats. The people are very dark; there are no fair ones.[104] The language is different from other countries. The inhabitants here are fond of eating lice, as they wear woolens which have many lice and nits. Whenever they catch one, they immediately put it into their mouths. They would never throw it away.

17. Lesser Bolor

From Kaśmīr I travelled further northwest for seven days, crossed the mountains, and arrived at the country of Lesser Bolor,[105] which is under Chinese rule. The dress, customs, food, and language are similar to those of Greater Bolor. The people wear cotton shirts[106] and boots, cut their beards and hair, and bind their heads with a piece of cotton cloth. Women keep their hair. The poor are many and the rich are few. The valleys are narrow and cultivable lands are limited. The mountains are withered and sterile[107], with no trees or grass. Greater Bolor was originally the place where the king of Lesser Bolor resided. It was because the Tibetans have come that he fled and shifted his residence to Lesser Bolor. The chiefs and common people remained and did not come [with the king].

18. Gandhāra

From Kaśmīr I travelled further northwest. After one month's journey across the mountains I arrived at the country of Gandhāra.[108] The king and military personnel are all Turks. The natives are Hu people; there are also Brahmins. The country was formerly under the influence of the king of Kāpiśa.[109] A-yeh, the Turkish prince, took a defeated cavalry and allied himself to the king of Kāpiśa. Later, when the Turkish force was strong, the prince assassinated the king of Kāpiśa and declared himself king. Thereafter, the territory from this country to the north[110] was all ruled by the Turkish king, who also resided in this country.[111]

The mountains are withered with no grass or trees. The dress, customs, language, and climate are all different [from other countries]. The dress includes furs, cotton shirts[112], boots, and trousers. The land is suitable for barley and wheat. There is no sorghum, millet, or rice. People mostly eat parched grain and pastry. Except for Kaśmīr, Greater and Lesser Bolor, and Yang-t'ung, the rest of the countries from Gandhāra to the five regions of India, and further to the Malay archipelago[113], all do not produce grapes[114], but only sugarcane.[115]

The Turkish king possesses five elephants and countless sheep and horses. Camels, mules, and asses are plentiful. [Because] China [fights] against the Hu[116] people one cannot go east without detour.[117] Towards the south the road is dangerous and difficult, and there are many bandits. From here to the north, evil occupations are many.[118] There are many butcheries in the towns' shops.

Though the king is of Turkish origin, he greatly believes and respects the Three Jewels. The king, the royal consort, the prince, and the chiefs build monasteries separately and worship the Three Jewels. The king institutes the great feast of the *Wu-che* assembly twice a year. Whatever he personally likes and uses-his wife, elephants, and horses-he donates [to the Saṅgha]. The king asks only that the monks fix the price of his wife and elephants, so that he can redeem them. As for the rest, the camels, horses, gold and silver, clothes, and furniture, are all sold by the monks. The amount is shared by the monks for their expenditures. These are the differences between this king and the other Turkish kings of the north. His sons and daughters act similarly, separately building monasteries, offering feasts, and giving donations.

The city[119] is built on the northern bank of the great Indus river. Three days' travel from this city to the west, there is a great monastery which was the residential monastery of *Bodhisattvas* Vasubandhu[120] and Asaṅga. The monastery is called Kaniṣka.[121] There is a great *stūpa* which constantly glows. The monastery and the *stūpa* were built by the former king Kaniṣka, so the monastery was named after him.

Southeast . . . *li* from this city is the place where the Former Buddha saved the dove for King Śibi. At present there are monasteries and monks. The place where the Former Buddha offered his head and eyes to the five *Yakṣas*[122] is also situated in this country. The places are all in the mountains southeast of the city. Each of these places has monasteries and monks, which are presently being supported. Both Mahāyāna and Hīnayāna are practised here.

19. Udyāna

From Gandhāra, going directly north, I entered the mountains, travelled for three days and arrived at the country of Udyāna, which its people call Uḍḍiyāna.[123] The king of this country greatly reveres the Three Jewels. Most of his villages and their inhabitants have been donated for the support of the monasteries. Only a few villages remain his own and even food and clothing from them are donated to the monasteries. He daily offers feasts [to the Saṅgha]. There are many monasteries and monks. There are slightly more monks than laymen. The dress, food, and customs here are similar to Gandhāra, though the languages are different. The land has many camels, mules, sheep, cotton clothing, and similar things. The climate is very cold.

20. Chitral

From Udyāna, after fifteen days journery travelling further northeast, I arrived at the country of Chitral which its people call Sha-mo-chieh-lo-che.[124] The king [of this country] also reveres and believes in the Three Jewels. There are many monasteries and monks. The dress and language are similar to those of Udyāna. The people wear cotton shirts and trousers. There are also sheep and horses.

21. Lampāka

Further to the west from Gandhāra, I entered the mountains, and after seven days journey arrived at the country of Lampāka.[125] The country has no king, but has a great chief. The country is also subject to Gandhāra. The dress and language are similar to those of Gandhāra. There are also monasteries and monks here. The Three Jewels are revered and believed. Mahāyāna Buddhism is practised.

22. Kapiśa

From Lampāka, I again entered the mountains. After eight days journery I arrived at the country of Kapiśa. This country is also under the authority of the king of Gandhāra. During the summer the king comes to Kapiśa and resides here because of the cool temperature. During the winter he goes to Gandhāra and resides at that warm place[126] because there is no snow and it is warm and not cold. In the winter the snows accumulate in Kāpiśa. This is the reason for the cold.

The natives of the country are Hu people; the king and the cavalry are Turks. The dress, language, and food of this place are mostly similar to Tokhāristan[127], though there are small differences. Whether man or woman, all wear cotton shirts, trousers, and boots. There is no distinction of dress between men and women. The men cut their beards and hair, but the women keep their hair. The products of this land include camels, mules, sheep, horses, asses, cotton cloth, grapes, barley, wheat, and saffron.

The people of this country greatly revere the Three Jewels. There are many monasteries and monks. The common people compete[128] in constructing monasteries and supporting the Three Jewels. In the big city there is a monastery called Sha-hsi-ssu.[129] At present, the curly hair[130] and the relic bones[131] of the Buddha are to be seen in the monastery. The king, the officials, and the common people daily worship these relics. Hīnayāna Buddhism is practised in this country. The land is situated in the mountains. On the mountains there is no vegetation. [It looks] as if the land had been burned by fire.

23. Zābulistān

From Kāpiśa I travelled further west and after seven days arrived at the country of Zābulistān[132] which its people call She-hu-lo-sa-t'a-na.[133] The native are Hu people; the king and cavalry are Turks. The king, a nephew of the king of Kāpiśa, himself controls his tribe and the cavalry stationed in this country. It is not subject to other countries, not even his own uncle. Though the king and the chiefs are Turks, they highly revere the Three Jewels. There are many monasteries and monks. Mahāyāna Buddhism is practised. There is a great Turkish chief called Sha-tuo-kan, who once a year lays out his gold and silver, which is much more than the king possesses. The dress, customs, and products of this land are similar to those of Kāpiśa, but the languages are different.

24. Bāmiyān

From Zābulistān I travelled further north and after seven days arrived at the country of Bāmiyān.[134] The king here is a Hu, and is independent of other countries. His cavalry is strong and numerous, and other countries dare not invade this land. The clothing consists of cotton shirts, furs, felt shirts and such. The products of this country include sheep, horses, and cotton. There are plenty of grapes. The land has snow and is extremely cold. The dwellings are mostly on the mountainside. The kings, the chiefs, and the common people highly revere the Three Jewels. There are many monasteries and monks. Both Mahāyāna and Hīnayāna are practised. The inhabitants of this country and those of Zābulistān cut their beards and hair. The dress is similar to that of Kāpiśa. Nevertheless, there are also many differences. The local dialects are different from those of other countries.

25. Tokhāristān

From Bāmiyān I travelled further north and after twenty days arrived at the country of Tokhāristān. The capital city is called Pactra.[135] At present, the place is guarded and oppressed by Arab forces. The original king was compelled to leave the capital[136], and he resided at Badakshan[137], which is one month's journey from the capital towards the east. It is also under the authority of the Arabs.

The language [of this country] is different from that of other countries. Though it is similar to the language of Kāpiśa, for the most part it is different. The dress is mostly made of fur, cotton, and similar things. From the king and chiefs down to the common people, all use fur as the outer garment. The land has many camels, mules, sheep and grapes. As far as food is concerned, the people are only fond of pastry. The land is cold. There is fog and snow during the winter. The king, the chiefs, and the common people respect the Three Jewels. There are many monasteries and monks. Hīnayāna Buddhism is practised. They eat meat[138], onions, and leeks. They do not profess any other religions. All men cut their beards and hair, but women keep their hair. The land is mountainous.

26. Persia

From Tokhāristān I travelled further west and after one month arrived at the country of Persia. Formerly, the king of this country ruled over the Arabs.[139] One Arab, the camel keeper[140] of the Persian king rebelled, assassinated the king, and declared himself the ruler. This is the reason why the country is now annexed by the Arabs.

The dress [or this country] is a wide cotton shirt. [The people] cut their beards and hair. They eat pastry and meat. Even if there is rice, they would grind it, make it into pastry, and then eat it. The products of the land are camels, mules, sheep, horses, big asses, cotton cloth, and precious articles. The languages is different from that of other countries.

The natives of this land are naturally skilful in trade.[141] They frequently sail to the western sea and enter the southern sea, and take precious things from the country of Ceylon. Thus, they claim that this land [Persia] produces all precious things by itself. They also take gold from the Malay archipelago, sail to Chinese territory, and proceed straight to Canton to buy silk gauze, silk wadding, and similar things. The land produces fine cotton. The inhabitants like to slaughter animals. They serve Heaven and have no knowledge of Buddhism.

27. Arabs

From the country of Persia,[142] I travelled further north and after ten days arrived at the country of the Arabs. The king of this country does not stay[143] on his own land. At present, he resides in Lesser Fu-lin[144] because he has conquered it. Moreover, that place is an island-like, strong fortress[145], which is the reason the king resides there.[146]

The products of this country are camels, mules, sheep, horses, cotton, woolen carpets, and precious things. The dress is a wide shirt made of fine cotton. Another piece of cotton added over the shirt is the outer garment. The king and the common people wear the same kind of clothing without distinction. Women also wear wide shirts.

Men cut their hair, but keep their beards. Women keep their hair.[147] When they eat food, there is no distinction between noble and commoner. They take food together from the same plate with their hands, and also use spoons and skewers.[148] They very much dislike taking ready-made things. They say that to eat the meat that is slaughtered by one's own hands brings boundless fortune. The inhabitants of this country are fond of slaughtering. They serve Heaven, and have no knowledge of Buddhism. In the law of the country, there is no convention of prostration.

29. Greater Fu-lin

Northwest of Lesser Fu-lin, along the sea shore, is the country of Greater Fu-lin.[149] The king has a very strong and large army. He is not subject to any other country. The Arabs made a few attacks, which did not succeed. The Turks also tried an invasion, which was also unsuccessful. The land has many precious things. Camels, mules, sheep, horses and such are very abundant. The dress is similar to that of Persia and the Arabs. The language is distinct from others.

29. Six Countries of Central Asia

From the country of the Arabs to the east, all the countries belong to the Hu people. These are the countries of Bokhara, Kaputana, Kish, Shih-lo, Maimarg, and Samarkand.[150] Though each of these countries has its own king, they are all under the authority of the Arabs. These countries are small, their armies are very limited, and they are unable to protect themselves. The products of these lands include camels, mules, sheep, horses, and cotton. The dress is cotton shirts, trousers, and furs. The languages are different from those of other countries.

Moreover, all these six countries serve the Fire Religion. They have no knowledge of Buddhism. Only in Samarkand is there one monastery and monk, who does not know how to revere [the Three Jewels]. In these countries of the Hu people, both the beard and hair are cut. People like to wear white caps made of cotton. One extremely bad custom is incestuous marriages, [which allows] one to take his own mother or sisters as his wives. The Persians also take their mothers as their wives. In the country of Tokhāristān and those of Kāpiśa, Bāmiyān, and Zābulistān, two, three, five, or even ten brothers are jointly married to one wife. They are not allowed to marry separately as they are afraid that separate marriages would ruin their livelihood.

30. Ferghana

To the east of Samarkand is the country of Ferghana[151] where they have two kings. The great Fu-yu river[152] flows to the west from the center of the country. The king to the south of the river is subject to the Arabs. The king to the north of the river is subject to the Turks. The products of the land include camels, mules, sheep, horses, and cotton cloth. The dress is made of fur and cotton. The food is mainly pastry and parched wheat. The language is different from that of other countries. The inhabitants have no knowledge of Buddhism. There are no monasteries, monks or nuns.

31. Khuttal

East of Ferghana there is a country called Khuttal. The king is of Turkish origin. Half of the local inhabitants are Hu people, and the other half are Turks. The products of this land include camels, mules, sheep, horses, cows, asses, grapes, cotton cloth, and woolen rugs. The dress is made of cotton and fur. The language is one-third Tokharian, one-third Turkish, and one-third local dialect. The kings, the chiefs, and the common people respect and believe the Three Jewels. Hīnayāna Buddhism is practised. This country is under the control of the Arabs. Although other countries call it a country, its size is only comparable with a great prefecture in China. The men of this country cut their beards and hair. The women keep their hair.[153]

32. Turks

From the country of the Hu people up to the northern sea in the north, the western sea in the west, and China[154] in the east, is the territory inhabited by the Turks. The Turks have no knowledge of Buddhism. There are no monasteries or monks. The dress is fur and woolen shirts. Insects are used for food.[155] There are no cities or houses. Felt tents are used for houses, which people carry with them wherever they go. The movement of the Turks follows the course of water and grass. The men cut their beards and hair. The women keep their hair.[156] The language is different from that of other countries. The people of this land are fond of killing. They do not distinguish between good and bad. The land has many camels, mules, sheep, horses and such.

33. Wakhān

From Tokhāristān I walked east for seven days and arrived at the city where the Wakhān king resides.[157] When I was at Tokhāristān, I met the Chinese Ambassador to foreign lands. I wrote a five-word poem in four rhymes, to express my feelings:

You complain that the way to the Western Barbarians is distant.
I lament for the long way east:
Barren roads on huge snowy ranges,
Dangerous torrents and bandits at every turn,
Flying birds are alarmed by the precipitous cliffs,
People are in danger walking on slanting bridges.[158]
I, who have never wept in my life,
Now shed a thousand tears.

[Another poem on the] snowy day at Tokhāristān in the five word style:

Cold snow becomes ice,
Cold winds crack the earth,
Great oceans of snow, frozen and extending far,

Rivers and streams erode the sides of the cliffs,[159]
Even the Dragon Gate waterfall becomes frozen.[160]
Wells seem to be covered by coiling snakes,
With fire I climb up the steps and sing.[161]
How can I cross the Pamirs?

The king of Wakhān has a small and weak cavalry and can not protect himself. At present he is under the authority of the Arabs. He pays annually three thousand rolls of silk to the Arabs. He is stationed in a valley which is narrow, and most people are poor. The dress is fur and woolen shirts. The king wears silk gauze and cotton cloth. Only pastry and parched wheat are used for food. The land is much colder than other countries. The language is different. The sheep and cows of this country are very small. There are also horses and mules. The monasteries and monks are there. Hīnayāna Buddhism is practised. The king, the chiefs, and the common people all serve Buddha and do not belong to other religions. This is the reason why other religions are not in this land. The men cut their beards and hair. The women keep their hair. The people live on the mountains where there are no trees[162], water, or grass.

34. Nine Shih-ni Countries

In the northern mountains of Wakhān there are nine Shih-ni[163] countries. Each of these nine kings commands his troops[164], and they are stationed [in one place]. One of them is subject to the king of Wakhān. The rest are independent and not subject to any other country. Recently there were two K'u kings who submitted to China, and messengers are continuously sent[165] to An-hsi. Only the king and chiefs wear cotton and furs; the rest of the common people wear fur and woolen shirts. The land is extremely cold, [people] make their homes on the snowy mountains. This is different from other countries. Here there are sheep, horses, cows, and donkeys. The language is different from that of other countries. The king often sends two to three hundred men to the valley of Ta-po-mi[166] to plunder the Hu traders as well as the messengers. Even if they took silk, they would pile it in storage rooms, and let it rot as they do not know how to make clothing. In these Shih-ni countries, Buddhism is not practised.

35. Ts'ung Ling

From Wakhān I travelled for another fifteen days towards the east, across the Po-mi valley and arrived at the garrison town of Ts'ung Ling.[167] The town is under Chinese control and Chinese troops are on guard here. Formerly, this was the territory of King P'ei-hsing[168], but that king rebelled against China, fled and submitted to the Tibetans. There are no inhabitants in this country at present. The foreigners call this place K'o-fan-t'an,[169] the Chinese name is Ts'ung Ling.

36. Kashgar

From Ts'ung Ling I travelled[170] another month and arrived at Kashgar.[171] The foreigners call this place Kashgiri.[172] The place is also guarded by Chinese troops.[173] There are monasteries and monks. Hīnayāna Buddhism is practised. People eat meat, onions, leeks, and such.[174] The local inhabitants wear cotton clothes.

37. Kucha

From Kashgar I travelled further east for one month and arrived at the country of Kucha.[175] This is the headquarters of the great protectorate of An-hsi,[176] the place where Chinese troops are gathered. In Kucha there are many monasteries and monks. Hīnayāna Buddhism is practised. The foods are meat, onions, leeks, and such. The Chinese monks practise Mahāyāna Buddhism.

38. Khotan

Two thousand *li* from An-hsi is the country of Khotan.[177] There are also many Chinese troops stationed here. There are many monasteries and monks. Mahāyāna Buddhism is practised. No monks eat meat.

From here eastward is all the territory of the Great T'ang empire. This is known to all. One can understand [the Situation] without further explanation.

39. Monasteries of An-hsi

I arrived at An-hsi during the first ten day period of the eleventh moon of the fifteenth year of the *K'ai-yüan* era.[178] At that time, the military governor was his excellency Chao.[179]

There are two monasteries presided over by Chinese monks.[180] They practise Mahāyāna Buddhism and eat no meat. The abbot of the Ta-yün monastery is Hsiu-hsing, who is well versed in discourse and speech. Previously, he was a monk of the Ts'i-pao-t'an Monastery in the capital. The Duty Distributor[181] called Yi-ch'ao understands the *Vinaya Piṭaka* very well.[182] Previously he was a monk of the Chuang-yen Monastery in the capital. The Chief Chair[183] of the Ta-yün Monastery[184] called

Ming-yün, who had a high moral character, originally came from the capital. These monks are good chiefs.[185] They possess religious determination and perform religious worship with joy.

The abbot of the Lung-hsing Monastery[186] is called Fa-hai. Though he is a Chinese born in An-hsi, his scholarship and manners are not different from those of China.

There is a Chinese monastery called Lung-hsing-ssu in Khotan. A Chinese monk called ... is the abbot of the monastery, and he is a good abbot. This monk is a native of Chi-chou in Ho-pei.

There is also a Chinese monastery called the Ta-yün-ssu in Kashgar. A Chinese monk resides over the monastery, who is a native of Min-chou.

40. Wu Chih

From An-hsi I travelled further east for ... and arrived at the country of Wu-chih.[187] The place is also guarded by Chinese troops. There is a king, and the inhabitants are Hu people. There are many monasteries and monks. Hīnayāna Buddhism is practised.

There are four towns in the An-hsi region[188], namely An-hsi [Kucha], Khotan, Kashgar, and Wu-chih... they follow Chinese customs. Around their heads they wear [turbans] ...

Notes To The Translation*

1. The MS. begins with this fragmentary account of a group of non-Buddhists. The three treasures are the Buddha, the Dharma, and the Saṅgha.

2. The character 衣, though faint, can be nothing else. (*Haneda Anniversary,* Vol. I, p. 627, note I.) Cf. Tokyo MS, 1a, line I.

3. "They have [no] slaves" [無] 有奴婢 (Fuchs). See the following sentence and MS, 4b, line 10, 無有奴婢. The absence of slavery in India impressed the Greek explorers who came with Alexander the Great–Strabo, *Geography* XV i 34, C 701 and 54, C 710; Arrian, *Indica* x 8–9. But Jan Yün-hua avers, "In the 8th century A. D. there were slaves in India. ' [Ed.] In agreement with Sadakata, we decided to translate,".... They have [no] slaves."

4. Kuśinagara 拘尸那國.

5. The place is called 'Māthā–kuär (Dead Prince) today by the locals.

6. 禪師 is a higher priest or monk, not a common monk.

7. The eighth of the Indian Eighth Month would be the fifteenth of the Far Eastern Seventh Month, according to Dr. So Kyong–bo of Dong–A University, Pusan, Korea. The fifteenth of the Seventh Month used to be celebrated in Korea as U–ran–bun–hoe; see Choe Sang–su, *Annual Customs of Korea,* Seoul, 1960, p. 75 f. 八月八日 refers to the month of Kārttika in the Indian Calenders. It is a Sarvāstivāda tradition.

8. Airāvatī–"The Ajitavatī 阿持多代底 of Hsüan–tsang, (Beal II, 32, footnote 89); according to him the *Stūpa* (tower) stood then westward of the river: probably this can be explained by a change in the course of the Ajitavatī." Cf. Fuchs, p. 431, note 6.

9. *Haneda Anniversary,* Vol. I, p. 627, note 2: "恒 in Fuchs is wrong." But in light of the fact that MS, Ia, line 7 has the same as Fuchs, it seems that the latter is correct after all.

10. "tigers" so Fuchs translater 大虫. [Ed.] Sadakata translates as 'ōgata no mushi or 'large insects.'

11. 娑般檀寺 [Ed.] According to Fujita, this is Makuta–Bandhana which appears in the *Māhaparinibbāna–sutta.*

12. "On the road ... sites"–reading in MS, only Ia, line 8, the faintly visible 有(卌餘之) 村庄三五所 not deciphered by Fuchs.

13. For 彼 read 波 (Fuchs). This is modern Benares.

14. The first five converts were Ajñāta–Kauṇḍinya 阿若憍陳如, Assaji 阿說示, Māhanāma 摩訶男, Bhaddiya 婆提, and Vappa 婆濕波. According to Dr. Zenryū Tsukamoto, director of the Kyoto Museum, Kyoto, Japan,

*This section is mainly the work of Prof. Yang except for the editorial notes indicated by [Ed.].

in a letter to H. S. Yang dated July 16, 1961, statues of these five are now preserved in the Calcutta Museum. *Indological Journal* (hereafter *IJ*), Vol. IV, Pt ii, Sept., 1968, p. 267: "The statues were perhaps erected after Hsüan-tsang's departure from India. Since archeological excavations have not unearthed these modelled statues, they might have perished or have been taken elsewhere." Cf. *Haneda Anniversary,* Vol. I, p. 627, note 4: "輸 in Fuchs is wrong." But Fuchs, p. 432, note 4: 彼五俱輸 corresponds to 拘驎等五人 Nothing like 輸 in Fuchs can be seen." Fuchs, p. 458: 輸.

15. 素 (em. Fuchs; 索 MS.) 形像・素＝塐＝塑 (Fuchs). *Haneda Anniversary,* Vol. I, p. 627, note 5: "It is 素." MS, Ia, line 11 has the same as Fuchs.

16. "beautiful" 麗 em. Fuchs; 麁 (＝麤 "rough, bulky") MS.

17. *IJ* p. 267: "... According to Hui-ch'ao, the pillar is an armful to five persons (sic). But at the time of the archeological excavations, F. O. Oettel found the column measured above 27 1/2' in height and it tapered from 2' 4" diameter at the bottom to I′ 10′′ diameter at the top.... At time of the excavations, the column was found a short distance to the west of the main shrine."

18. *IJ*, p. 268, and 269: ".... According to Hsüan-tsang, the monastery at Sarnath could be named as Mṛgadava Sanghārama. This name has been translated by S. Beal as the Sanghārama of Lu-ye ('Stag desert'); hence Li Yung-hsi rendered the name as the Deer Park Monastery."

19. *IJ,* p. 269: "This statement of 'wear no cloth and smear ashes on their bodies' are identical with Hsüan-tsang's record. In the travels of Fa-hsien, though it was stated that there are now two monasteries in the deer forest, both with resident priests, the name of the monastery is not mentioned. In the archeological reports, the monastery has been described as the main shrine or Mūlagandhakuti. Now in the memoir of Hui-ch'ao, it is clearly recorded that the monastery was called Ta-mo-kan-ko-lo-seng, which leaves no doubt of its being a transliteration from the original Sanskrit name Dharmacakra-sanghārama. Though Fujita Toyohachi has in his commentray of the *Memoir* agreed that the monastery should be named as Dharmacakra-sanghārama, he has a long discussion which aims to identify the name with Dhamekha-stūpa."

20. *Haneda Anniversary,* Vol. I, p. 627, note 7: "事於大天 should be continued 此寺中." But Fuchs has 事於大天下缺. MS. 1a, line 14 is not so clear but it seemed to be right. According to *Bulkyo sajun,* p. 163, 大天 is Mahādeva. In B. C. 4 he was in India. Conspiring with his mother, he killed his father. an Arhat 羅漢. After that, he understood Buddhist doctrines; pretending to be a Buddhist, he did not believe in Buddha. *IJ* p. 269: ".... Hui-ch'ao s reference to Śiva worship at the place corroborates the statement of Hsüan-tsang, the only difference being about the location of this worship. Hsüan-tsang says that at Vārāṇasī he found a hundred or so

Deva temples with about 10,000 sectaries. They honor principally Maheśvara. In the memoir of Hui–ch'ao, the worship is mentioned in the course of the account concerning both Vārāṇasī proper and Sarnath."

21. Cf. *Bulkyo sajun,* p. 178 and *Bukkyo daijiten,* Vol. 5, p. 4727. The 獨覺像 in Fuchs, p. 432, note 9 is based on an emendation by Takakusu, *YHD*, p. 5. ' *IJ,* pp. 269–270: "This is perhaps a reaffirmation of Hsüan–tsang's reference. In the shrine hall there was a life size bronze image of Buddha in the attitude of turning the wheel of law."

22. Fuchs, p. 432, note 10: "D. I. Harṣavardhana, 608–647; er war Kanyuakubia, hatte sich aber ganz Mittel–Indien mit Magada unterwerfen... Fuchs, p. 432 and 458 changes 尸羅票底 to 尸羅粟底, but the manuscript is not clear. *IJ*, p. 270," The mention of Buddhist statues and a gift wheel made by King Śīlāditya is very significant. Though Hsüan–tsang informs us about Harṣa's devotion to Buddhism and his patronage to Buddhists and though we are also told that Harṣa had erected thousands of *topes* on the bank of the Ganges and Buddhist monasteries at the sacred places of the Buddhists .... there has been no indication about his making statues. On this point the information contained in the Memoir has enriched our knowledge on the great ruler of Kanuij. Since Hsüan–tsang was a personal friend of Harṣa, he would not have missed recording the fact if the latter had been making the statues of Buddha at Sarnath.... In the *Memoir,* Hui–ch'ao addressed Harṣa as a former king of Magadha. This tallies with the official records of the History of T'ang dynasty."

23. This is an old kingdom of Middle India. This country had the deepest relation with Buddhism. The first book of Buddhist doctrine was made in this country. Cf. *Bulkyo sajun.* p. 195.

24. Fuchs, p. 432, note II, and p. 458 has 輻團正寸卅餘步 but *Haneda Anniversary,* Vol. I, p. 627, note 8: "輻團正寸卅餘步 is wrong; and it would be 輻團等寸卅餘步" However, 輻團正寸卅餘步 in Tokyo MS agrees with Fuchs. *IJ,* p. 266: "... thirty and odd spaces in diameter."

25. 四大靈塔：佛生處，成道處，初轉法輿處，人涅槃處.

26. □□得達摩訶菩提寺.

27. These are the eight holy places where Gautama preached while travelling. The four above–mentioned holy places are said to give blessings to the human world; the other four spiritual places to give blessings from heaven. This is why eight towers were established. See *Bukkyo daijiten,* Vol. 5, p. 4220. Cf. Fuchs, p. 433, note 8: "An den acht in Buddhas leben wichtigen Statten erbaut; vgl. Oda, p. 1410 s. v. t."

28. *Haneda Anniversary,* Vol. I, p. 627, note 9: "In the original document there is 難誠見, but it should be read as 誠難見. " In Tokyo MS, Ib, line 7 (MS, p. 164) has the same as 難誠見. However, the right order should be 誠難見.

29. *Haneda Anniversary,* Vol. I, p. 627, note 10: "參著經 should be 參差經. There is 參差 in 慧林一切經音義中の音義 as evidence." In Tokyo MS, Ib, line 參著經 can be faintly seen. *IJ*, p. 266 translated 參著經 as 'marks of kalpa'.

30. *IJ,* p. 272: "In the archeological report Cunningham states: "It will have been observed that every excavation made near Sarnath has revealed traces of fire, I myself found charred timber and half-burnt grain. The same things were also found by Major Kittoe. So vividly was the impression of a great final catastrophe by fire fixed in Major Kittoe's mind by the discoveries made during his excavations that he thus summed up his conclusions to me in a few words: 'All has been sacked and burnt, priests, temples, idols, all together. In some places, bones, iron, timber, idols, etc. are all fused into huge heaps; and this has happened more than once.' According to some scholars, the place might have been burnt down by the Huns when they invaded northern India during the 5th and 6th century of the Christian era, while Belgar and others are of the opinion that the Buddhist monuments might have suffered from the fury of the Moslem conquerors."

31. Fuchs, p. 433 translated "Wie kann da mein Wunchgelübde erfüllt wer?" A literal translation would be: "How could a person's desire be fulfilled?"

32. Kānyakubja (Pāli, Kaṇṇakujja). Cf. Mizutani, pp. 161–162. footnote 1 and 2.

33. Tokyo MS, 1b, line 8 has 百姓繁閑. But *Haneda Anniversary*, Vol. I, p. 627, note II has "鬧 is right." However, Fuchs, p. 434, note 1 has the same as 鬧.

34. *Journal of Indian History* (hereafter *JIH*), Vol. XLV, Part I, No. 133, April 1967, p. 167: "Although no name of this central (Middle) Indian king is given by the Sillian king, since the time of his visit was about 723–724 A. D., the powerful ruler whom he described should have been no other than Yaśovarman, a historical person, who could not achieve the great glory of World Conquest.... Yaśovarman, sending his minister Bhadanta Po–ta–hsin to the Chinese Emperor, Hsüan–tsang of the T'ang dynasty, prayed for diplomatic recognition."

35. In Tokyo MS, Ib, line 11, 唯南天村草百姓語有（？）差別. Fuchs, p. 458 interprets as 有. *Oriens Extremus,* December, 1968, p. 177: "The Sanscrit language, although already used in official circles, had not yet penetrated into the root of South Indian society. Many of the local languages of the Chalukyan kingdom linguistically belonged to the Dravidian group."

36. Tokyo MS, Ib, line 13 has 形戮. *Haneda Anniversary,* Vol. I, p. 628, note 12: "形 should be corrected as 刑." Likewise, Fuchs, p. 459.

37(傷 'hurt', em. Fuchs; 殤 'die away', MS (Ib. 14).

38. Fuchs, p. 434, note 8 has 懷物 to 情物. *Haneda Anniversary,* Vol.

I, p. 628, note 12: "In the original manuscript there is 怯, but it should be 怯." I follow Fuchs because 情 makes better sense; 怯 means 'fear'. 情 is more intelligible than 怯.

39. Fuchs, p. 434: "Brotkuchen und gedampfte Teigwaren." that is, 'rice–cake' and 'roasted rice or bariey ground into flour. Cf. Fuchs, p. 434, note 10. Actually in Korean 餅麨 is "Ttuk" 떡 and "Misit karu 미싯가루, Roosted rice or barley is ground into a powder for 麨. Cf. *Hanhan desajun,* p. 128.

40. Fuchs, p. 434: "乳酪蘇 means Schmelzbutter, Milch und Sahne."

41. [Ed.] Fuchs, p. 436, note 2 corrects 似於漠屋雨下作也 to 似於漢屋雨下作也, In Tokyo MS. 2a, line 10 has the same as 似於漠屋雨下作也. It is because 似於漠屋雨下作也 does not make sense. It still, however, does not make good sense to say, ".... similar to the Chinese house built at the time of rains." In agreement with Sadakata, we read 雨 as 兩. Thus, our trauslation" .... similar to the Chinese house (i. e., gabled)."

42. Anāthapiṇḍika 給孤園 was a mile away from Śrāvastī. This was the place where the Buddha Gautama preached. See Fuchs, p. 436 and *Bulkyo sajun,* p. 107.

43. Śrāvastī 舍衛國 was a town in Kosala country in Middle India. When Buddha was alive, the kings Pasesādi and Virudhaka lived here and a famous Jetavana–vihara also existed. This location was known as Stemaht in today's Conda after discovering the relic. See p. 37, *Bulkyo sajun* 불교사전.

44. Fuchs, p. 460 has 毘耶離城 but in Tokyo MS, 2b, line I the characters 毗耶離城 can be seen. Cf. *Bulkyo sajun,* p. 34: Vaiśālī was in Middle India on the Ganges river. When Gautama was alive, he used to visit here.

45. Fuchs, p. 460 has 迦毘耶羅國 but Tokyo MS, 2b, line 2 has 迦毗耶羅國. Kapilavastu is in the area of Tarai in Nepal. This was the place where Gautama was born. See *Pyojun Kukue sajun* 標準國語辭典. p. 10

46. north (北) em. Fuchs, 比 (sic) MS. (2b 3).

47. *Sandō no Hōkai,* cf. Mochizuki *Bukkyo Daijiten* vol. L, p. 1627. Three lanes of jewels, gold, silver and agate, were magically created by the god Indra of the *Tusita* Heaven in order to 'pave' the way for the Buddh who was returning from the *Tusita* Heaven to the world after preaching to his mother, Queen Māyā. This is represented on the Bhārūt and Sanchi *torāna* (gate-way) reliefs. [Ed.]

48. *Trayastriṃśa* is the second of the six heavens. See *Bukkyō daijiten,* Vol. 4, pp. 3920–21 and *Bulkyo sajun,* p. 170.

49. Jambudvipa 閻浮提 is the continent to the south of Mount Sumeru on which our world is located. See *Bulkyo sajun,* p. 589.

50. Brahma is the supreme god of the Hindus. The word Brahman, is used for the highest principle of the universe.

51. The king of *Trayastriṃśa* 帝釋 controls 4000 kings and 32 heavens

and protects the people who want to become Buddhists. See *Bulkyo sajun*, p. 788. According to Junjiro K. Takakukusu "Śākra 帝釋 in India is treated as a God but Śākra in Persia is treated as a devil. ' See *Bukkyō no shinzui* 佛教の眞髓 (Dai ichi shōbō,. Tokyo, 1937), pp. 16–17.

52. Fuchs, p. 460 has 有寺有僧 but Tokyo MS, p. 4, line 7 (MS, plate 2 b 7) has 有寺僧有. I follow Fuchs because 有寺有僧. is the right order.

53. In the Tokyo MS, 2b, line 7, 至南天竺國王所住 can be clearly seen, But Fuchs added "住".

54. Presumably, this is Vatapi, that is Badami, capital of the Western Chalukyas. At the time of Hye Ch'o's visit to 'South India', this was the preeminent dynasty of the region. However, there is still very little that would prevent us interpreting Hye Ch'o to be referring to the Eastern Chalukyas of Vengi in the Andhra delta region. Perhaps the the solution of the problem hinges on the identity of the three-storeyed monastery mentioned in this section. If, as is suggested in note 56, this monastery was in lower Andhra, then the Eastern Chalukyas are *perhaps* indicated. On the other hand, if the three-storeyed monastery can be identified with the 'Don Thal' and/or 'Tin Thal' of Ellora (both three-storeyed rock-cut monasteries excavated at least a century before our pilgrim's visit), then this may give a better claim to the identification of the Western Chalukyas. In essence, the problem is unsolvable given the brevity of Hye Ch'o's statements. [Ed.]

55. MS. 2b, line 11, 王及首領百姓等. Sadakata suggests a reading of 領首 here. Either way, one can get the meaning of chiefs .

56. [Ed.] According to both Fa Hsien and Hsüan–tsang, there was a cave temple called Bhramarā (跋邏末羅 which means 黑蜂). Bhramarā or 'Black bee is a name of Durgā, Pāravatī. The cave temple actually exists today in the mountain of Undavilli near Bezwada. As noted by Sadakata, the hill is still called 'black hill' (Telegu Malla-Malai) by the locals.

57. MS, 2b, line 13 has 便夜叉. Fuchs, p. 460 changes 便夜叉 to 使夜叉. We follow Fuchs because 便 means good or convenient. 便 does not make sense here. 使 means "let" or "make". So 使 makes better sense.

58. [Ed.] Regarding this costly endeavour of building a cave temple complex, that Nāgārjuna's plea was not to Yakṣa, but instead to a certain Sātavāhana king in his *Suhṛlleka*.

59. Fuchs, p. 437 "15 piku (etwa 1800) pfc)." 15 *picul* is about 2000 lbs.

60. Fuchs, p. 438 nach China," but we think 鄉 is the area of Kyungjoo, the capital of Silla. Hye Ch'o might have been born in this area.

61. Fuchs, p. 438 interpretes 日南 as Annam or Vietnam. However, according to the Korean sinologist U–sung Yi," 日南 is a hot place in China, not Annam. Korea and Japan are called as 日東. (oral communication). Jan Yün–hua does not agree. Could 日南 mean "south of the (summer) sun",

i. e. south of the Tropic of Cancer?

62. "geese" 雁 em. Fuchs; "hawks" 鷹 MS. In South India hawks are plentiful but geese do not exist. Since Hye Ch'o's complaint is that the bird he wants is lacking, "geese" would be more likely. A scribe could easily mistake 雁 or 鴈 and then substitute the equivalent character 鷹 to display his learning. *Haneda Anniversary,* Vol. I, p. 628, note 15:" 鷹 can be seen, but if it is a hawk, it is difficult to understand the meaning of the poetry. Therefore, 'geese' in Fuchs would be better."

63. Fuchs, p. 438 interpretes 林 "grove" but it should be translated as 'my home. Perhaps 林 is an abbreviation of 鷄林. *Samkuk-saki* translated with notes by Dr. Byung Do Yi, p. 271, (Vol. 2, October, 1957) "熊川州 was abbreviated as 熊州 and 武珍州 was abbreviated as 武州."

64. Fuchs, p. 438, note 3: "Bemals Dahir, der im Jahre 712 von den Arabern durch Muhanned ibn Kasim verichtet; seine drei Sohne versuchten, die Herrschaft wieder herzustellen, wurden jedoch auch im Jahre 725, also gerade zur Zeit der Reise von Huei-ch'ao, verhichtet; cf. Smith, p. 369."

65. MS. 3a, line 7 has 此西天王亦五六百頭象. which Fuchs corrects to 此西天王有亦五六百頭象. We follow Fuchs here.

66. Fuchs, p. 438: Arabia

67. Fuchs, p. 439, note 2: "Vgl. Beal I, 175–77; YHD, 14 liest falsch 闍." cf. p. 430 of Fuchs. Jālandhara.

68. Fuchs, p. 461 and p. 430: Kashmir.

69. Fuchs, p. 461 corrects 所有出象 to 所出有象. *Haneda Anniversary,* Vol. I, p. 628, note 17: "所有出 is incorrect. 所出有 is right." MS, 3b, line 5 has 所有出象.

70. Fuchs, p. 439, note 5: "YHD liest falsch 土番國." MS, 3b, line 7 has 土蕃.

71. MS, 3b, line 8 has 社吒國. Fuchs, p. 439, note 6: "社吒國 lies 吒社, das 石祭迦 chih-chia von Hsüan-tsang (Beal I, 16) und das Tashar (Takin, Tafan) der Araber im Heutigen Panjab." *Haneda Anniversary,* Vol. I, p. 628, note 18: "社吒 is reversed for 吒社."

72. Fuchs, p. 440, note 1: "Nach der Beschreibung vielleicht Bajputana. Da Hsüan-tsang (Beal II, 269–270) in dieser Gegend das Reich Gurjjara 瞿折羅 nennt, ist 古羅 wohl dafur dialektisch."

73. *Bulkyo sajun,* p. 812: "saṅghabhadra 衆賢論師 was from northern Kashmir; he wrote the *Nyāyānusāraśāstra* 順正理論 and argued with 天親菩薩."

74. See Oda *Bukkyō jiten,* p. 32 (194) and *Bulkyo sajun,* p. 497 and p. 552.

75. MS, 3b, line 14 has 得色得力. Fuchs, p. 440, note 4: "MS und T. T. lesen 得色; YHD 17, falsch 得氣 得色得力 means 'become lively and eager for action.'

76. Fuchs, p. 440, note: "Im MS muss hier die Zeitangabe ausgefallen

sein."

77. Fuchs, p. 440, note 6: "Hsüan–tsang (Beal I, 173) umschreibt as 答林蘇代所 sudwestlich von Jālandhara."

78. Fuchs, P. 461 changes 即佛所剃頭及剪爪 to (而) 即佛所剃頭剪爪. Fuchs, p. 440, note 7: "MS hat 口佛所剃頭, T. T. gibt fur 口; 而; YHD lasst 所 aus und gibt ver 佛 auch 而, offenbar aber unrightig im MS nicht deutlich Zu erkennen." However, 而 in the Ms. 4a, line 3, can be seen.

79. 大辟支 means "a person who realizes Buddhahood by himself, without learning Buddhist doctrine This is the same as 獨覺像." See *BS,* p. 286

80. Fuchs, p. 440, note 9: "大好住持 vgl, unten, p. 457, Anm 3 and Oda, 1227." [Ed.], 大好住持 can also be rendered as, "thing are great and good for boarding and lodging." Sadakata translates, "*ōini jin-seikatsu o aikōshiteiru* or "greatly enjoying the temple life".

81. Bhadanta 大德 originally meant Buddha; it also refers to the Buddhist doctrine. Sometimes priests who have great virtues and wisdom are callled Bhadanta.

82. MS, 4a, line 8 one spare has 玉皃. Fuchs, p. 462 and 441, note 2 changes 皃 to 貌. 皃 means a child, but 貌 means a figure or body. Therefore, we follow Fuchs. According to Jan Yün–hua, "The person which Hui ch'ao referred to was a Chinese monk (Han–seng), who died before Hye Ch'o s arrival at Nagaradhana. Hye Ch'o did not meet the monk, but heard of the misfortune from other members of the monastery." Cf. Fuchs, p. 462; Fujita 27a.

83. *Oriens Extremus,* p. 176: "At this time the missions that arrived at the T'ang court in 720 and 733 A. D., respectively, were for the Chinese recognition of the newly enthroned kings of Kashmir. The King of Kashmir, in 713 A. D., when the Korean general Ko Hsien Chih was alive, applied to the Chinese Emperor for aid against the Arabs.

84. MS, 4a, line 11 has 枝. Fuchs, p. 462 changes 枝 to 支二苦. 枝 means 'branch of a tree, but 支 means "carry or hold." We follow Fuchs.

85. MS, 4a, line 12 has 少馬. Fuchs, p. 462 changes 少馬 to 小馬. Because 少馬 means a few horses, according to the context 少馬 does not make sense. So it must be a small horse following Fuchs correction.

86. Fuchs, p. 462 translates 蒲桃 as grape. Today Koreans call the grape "p'odo" using the early pronunciation of 蒲桃 葡萄. This would be 吏讀文字.

87. MS, 4a, line 13 has 霜雨. Fuchs, p. 462 changes 霜雨 to 霖雨. 霜 means 'frost', and frost does fall in autumn, not in summer. 霖 is right. Cf. Fuchs, p. 441, note 7. So does Fujita.

88. MS, 4a, line 13 has 彫. Fuchs, however, in p. 462 changes 彫 to 稠. 彫 means "Draw or trim, ' but 稠 means "thick." 稠 is right.

89. *Bulkyo sajun,* p. 640: "龍王 lives in the sea, controls rain and water,

and protects Buddhists." Sometimes it means the people who control water.

90. MS, 4b, line 2 has "千一羅漢僧," but Fuchs, p. 442, note 1 corrects this to "一千羅漢僧." The order of 一千羅漢僧 is right. Cf. Fuchs, p. 442: Nāgarāja eintausend Lohan und Mönchen."

91. *Haneda Anniversary,* Vol. I, p. 628, note 20: "至國王王妃王子 is correct." However, Fuchs, p. 462: "至國 Fälschlich verdoppelt 王王妃王子." MS, 4b, line 5 has the same as Haneda: 至國" 王王妃王子. Fuchs, p. 462 changes 及妃姤 to 及妃后. MS, 4b, line 8 has the same as 及妃姤. Because 妃姤 does not make sense, 妃后 means king's wife and it makes sense.

93. MS, 4b, line 8 has 布施自由不王也 Fuchs, p. 462 changes 布施自由不王也 to 布施自由不問王也 In view of the context, Fuchs is correct.

94. MS, 4b, line 9 has 怕拈罪. Fuchs, p. 462 changes 怕佔罪 to 怕佔罪. 拈 means "take" but 佔 means "nears." In view of the context, 佔 would be better.

95. Fuchs, p. 463 changes 大勃律國 to 大勃律國. Fuchs, p. 443, note I: "Lies 大勃律國 as auch in Tang–shu; vgl. Chavannes, Dec., 1491, das 鉢盧勒 des Sung yung (Chav. Song Yun, 406 , Beal I, p. XCXII) und des Hsüan–tsang (Beal II, 289–90), heute Baltistan."

96. Fuchs, p. 443, note 2: "T. T. liest 楊; MS undeutlich, doch aber, wie weiter unten, 楊; das ist das 羊同 des T'ang–shu (大 und 小羊同國). Lage unsicher; das letztere lag wohl in der Gegend des heutigen Gyangtse (Shigatse) in Sud–Tibet, Vgl. auch Bushell, The early History or Tibet, JRSA Oct., 1880. p. 527, Anm. 9."

97. Fuchs, p. 443, note 3: "Lies 婆, im 一切經音義 durch 婆籛慈 umschrieben, was dem tib, h'bras spungs entspricht. Vgl. Levi, *Le Nepal* I, 1905, p. 186, und YHD, p. 21."

98. *Haneda Anniversary,* Vol. I:., pp. 697–698: 胡 may be 旡 or 女眞族 or 契丹. Fuchs, p. 443, note 5: "D. h. aus Tokharistan und benachbarten Ländern stammende Völker, Vgl. Chavannes, Rel. Émin., p. 13)."

99. *Dai hyakka jiten,* (Tokyo, 1933), pp. 197–198: "突厥 started from the Altai mountains. In the 6th Centery A. D. T'uküh was in present Russian territory near the Dar–ya river."

100. MS, 5a, line 4 has the character of 毡 which is faintly seen. Fuchs, p. 463 changes 毡褐之類 to 毯褐之類. 毡 must be 毯.

101. Fuchs, p. 443 translates 餠飯 as "Teigwaren und gekochte Reis." but in Korean it means a rice or wheat cake called (ttŏk) and boiled rice or boiled barley which is called "pap."

102. Fuchs, p. 443, note 7: "Nach der Tibet–Beschreibung im T'ang–shu, 256–57, spielte aber der Buddhismus damals schon eine Rolle; vgl. Bushell, "Early History or Tibet", JRAS 1880, p. 442. [Nach der chinesischen Überlieferung wurde der Buddhismus in Tibet durch die chinesischen Prin-

zessin Wen–tsch'eng eingeführt, die im jahre 641 mit König Srong–btsan sgam–po verheiratet wurde. Auch seine andere Gemahlin, ein nepalesische Prinzessin, dürfte daran nicht unbeteiligt gewesen sein. Franke.]

103. MS, 5a, line 5 has the character 抗. Fuchs, however, (p. 463) changes 抗而臥 to 坑而臥. 抗 means "oppose" or "challenge," but 坑 means "dig." In view of the context, 坑 is correct.

104. MS, 5a, line 6 has 白者全布. Fuchs, p. 463, note 5 changes 白者全布 to 白者全希. 白者全布 means "Whites are all cloth" but 白者全希 means "All whites are rare." According to the context, 白者全希 is correct.

105. Fuchs, p. 444, note 5: "D. i. der Distrikt von Gilgit, mit der Haupstadt Yashin; vgl. Chavannes, T'P. 1904, p. 43' und Song Yun, p. 406."

106. Fuchs, p. 44, note 6: "疊氎衫衫 see p.85 shan ist hier und im folgenden immer durch Oberkleidung wiedergegeben. Es bedeute eine kurze, einfache Art von Tunica; auch die Übersetzung Hemd ist möglich."

107. MS, 5a, line 10 has 惟衫. Fuchs, p. 463 changes 惟鬭 to 惟杭. 惟 means "think" But 熣 means "burn," and 杭 means "tree," In view of he context, 熣杭 is correct. Cf. Fuchs, p. 444, note 7.

108. Ghandhāra 建馱羅 is located in north–western India. Gandhāra sculpture is realistic, with the face and hair Western in style; the area was Buddhist under Kaniṣka after Alexander the Great's conquest. Cf. Fuchs, p. 444, note 9.

109. Fuchs, p. 444: "Kaniṣka (罽賓 nordest–Afghanistan)"

110. Fuchs, p. 463: "Die vier felgenden Zeichen gehören pleonastisch hinter."

111. MS, 5b, line 3 has 並住中. Fuchs, p. 463 changes 並住中 to 並住山中. We follow Fuchs because 並住中 means "all live in the middle," but 並住山 means "all live in the middle of the mountains." Therefore, in view of the context, 並住中 does not make sense.

112. MS, 5b, lines 2–3 have 皮毬氎. Fuchs, p. 463, note 11 changes 皮毬氎 to 皮毬二袭氎 We follow Fuchs because 毬 is not to be found

113. See *Tsui-hsing Han-yang wu-yung ta-tu-tieu,*(Nov., 1964), pp. 317–318.

114. Fuchs, p. 464 changes 總無蒲□□□ to 總無蒲桃唯有. Even in MS, 5b, line 4 and 5 three characters are missing after 總無蒲. We agree with Fuchs annotation in view of the context.

115. [Ed.] Although MS, 5b, line 6 has 曰, this is read as a part of the character 甘, which is followed by the character 蔗. Thus, 甘蔗 or sugarcane. Fuchs does the same (p. 464).

116. MS, 5b, line 5 has 甚漢多地 but Fuchs, p. 464 changes this 甚漢多地 to 甚多漢地 But we change it and add 漢地與胡.

117. Fuchs, p. 445, note 6: "MS beschadigt es feblen 3 Zeichen." Cf. MS, 5b, line 6 lacks five characters, too. For these five characters missing we

supplied 戰而不歸東.

118. bad occupations 惡業 em. Otani and Takakasu; 西業 MS. See Fuchs, p. 445 n. 7.

119. Fuchs, p. 466, note 1: "Vgl. Beal 1, 109. Da hier dan im folgenden erwähnte Kaniṣka–Kloster als westlich drei Tagereisen weit von der Hauptstadt entfernt angegeben ist, und da es andererseits nach Hsüan–tsang (Beal 1, 109) vom Kaniṣka-Kloster 50 li nordöstlich bis zur Stadt Puskalawati waren, muss hier als Hauptstadt diese letzte gemeint sein und nicht Puruspura (Peshawar)."

120. Vasubaudhu 天親菩薩 was born in Peshawar c. A. D. 400 Asaṅga 无着菩薩 was the younger brother of Vasubandhu.

121. *Bulkyo sajun,* p. 7: "Kaniṣka was of the 月氏, race and established Gandhāra."

122. 捨頭捨眼餧王夜叉 refers to the *Jataka* in which Gautama, before becoming a Buddha, was tested by Śākra 帝釋 and Brahma 波羅門 to see whether he would become a Buddha or not. Gautama was the king of Śibi 尸毘; Śākra became a pigeon. When the pigeon flew to the king of Śibi while being chased by an eagle, the king, without killing the pigeon, let it fly away. Cf. *Bulkyo sajun,* p. 372: "In order to practice the benevolence of a Bodhisttava, he offered his body to be killed."

123. Udyāna 烏仗那 is an area whose location has been ascribed to much of northern India. See *Bulkyo sajun,* p. 618.

126. Fuchs, p. 447, note I: "Das 拘緯 von Wu–k'ong, p. 348[1], in der Gegend von Tchitral und Mastuji; Chavannes, Notes Add., p. 43[2], 74[2]."

125. Fuchs, p. 447, note 3: "Gleich dem 濫波國 von Hsüan–tsang (Beal I, 90) und dem 藍婆國 des Wu–k'ong, 3482); das heutige Lamghan. T. T. Liest 波 statt 彼; MS undeutlich."

126. MS, 6a, line 10 has 趂暖而住. which Fuchs, p. 465 corrects to 趁暖而住. 趂 means "run" but 趁 means "follow." The latter makes more sense, meaning "following the warmth, (they) live."

127. Shiratori Kokichi, *Dozai koshoshiron* 東西交涉史論. Tokyo Imperial University, Shigakukai 史學界. Fuzambo, Tokyo, p. 7: "Tocharistan is the Turkish race and ancestors of the T'ukuh." Cf. *Dai hyakka jiten,* Vol. 10, pp. 60–61: "Tocharistan is a dead language in Central Asia. The dialect is Kucha."

128. [Ed.] MS. 6b, line 1 has 百姓家各絲造寺. The character 絲 poses a problem here. Fuchs takes this as 慈 (p. 465); *Haneda Anniversary* vol. I, p. 628, note 27: "Is it 竝 ?" 竝 (i. e., 並) means 'side by side'. Fujita says, "絲恐競之略". By following Fujita, we translate, "in competition". As Sadakata notes, 百姓家 or 'the common folk', can be construed as not being the subject of the sentence, but is instead an object of the sentence due to a possible mistake by the copyist of the manuscript.

129. [Ed.] Fuchs, p. 405 corrects 名沙糸寺 to 名沙糸寺. Fuchs, p. 448. note 3: "Dies ist eigentlich der Name der dortigen Dynastie (vgl. Ou–K'ong, 381). MS. T. T. und YHD lesen ungenau 糸 fur 系. "If we follow Sadakata's note, however, there is a possibility of 沙糸 as a transliteration of *śāhi,* which is an epithet of the Turkish (突厥) kings.

130. [Ed.] MS. 6b, line 2 has 寺中貝佛 but Fuchs, p. 465 added 有 as 寺中有貝佛. We however, take this as, "... of the Buddha".

131. 舍利 is Buddha's relics (Gautama's relics) or holy person's relics. See *Bulkyo sajun,* p. 359.

132. Ms. 6b, lines 4–5 have 西行至七日謝颶國 but Fuchs, p. 465, line II, center has 西行七日至謝颶國. We follow Fuchs because 西行七日至謝颶國 in Fuchs is the right order.

133. Fuchs, p. 448, note 5: "Vgl. Doc. 160–161; Eransahr, p. 247 ff. Zur Transkription von Hsieh–yu vgl. Pelliot, T'P. XXVI, 1928, p. 186." Cf. *Sekai dai hyakka jiten,* Vol. 12, pp. 168–169.

134. *Teihon sekai rekishi jizu* 定本世界歷史地圖, (Tokyo: Yoshikawa Kobunkan Co.), pp. 38–39: "犯引國 is in Afghanistan." Cf. Fuchs, p. 448, note 9.

135. Fuchs, p. 449, note I: "D. i. das 縛底野 des T'ang–shu (Doc., p. 162) und das 薄提 des Wei–shu Eransahr, p. 214–216; Doc., p. 1554)."

136. MS, 6b, line 13 has 其王被其王被逼, but Fuchs, p. 466 corrected corrected 其王被其王被逼 to 其王被逼. Fuchs, p. 466, note 2: "Versehentlich verdoppelt." In addition, Fuchs, p. 449, note 2: "Im Jahre 667 waren die Araber in Khorasan und Tokharistan eingefallen: der geflohene könig ist offenbar A–shih–na Wu–shih–po 阿史那烏濕波 (Doc., p. 157) aus der Mitte des 7. Jahrhunderts."

137. Fuchs, p. 449, note 3: "MS hat richtig 特, YHD falsch 持; gleich dem 勃特山 des 册府元龜 (Doc., 201) und dem 拔特山 des T'ang–shu (Doc., 69) Badakhschan. Die Entfernung von Balkh nach Badakhschan ist hier Übertrieben; nach Abulfeda betrug sie nur 13 Tagesreisen."

138. MS. 7a, line 5 has 食內. Fuchs, p. 466 corrected 食內 to 食肉. I follow Fuchs. Because 內 means "inside," In view of the context it does not make sense. In addition, 悲 is to be corrected to 韮. 悲 can not be found but 韮 can be the name of a vegetable. Fuchs, p. 449, note 5 explained "MS hat 內及葱韮 lies 肉及葱韮; die 2 letzten Zeichen sind im YHD nicht richtig erkannt."

139. MS. 7a, line 5 has 大々寔々. *Haneda Anniversary,* Vol. I, p. 628, note 28 has the same as 大々寔々. Fuchs divided this 大寔 and 大寔. In view of the context, Fuchs is correct.

140. MS. 7a, line 5 has 放馳戶 but Fuchs, p. 466 corrected 放馳戶 to 放駝戶. Because 馳 means "run," 放馳戶 does not make sense in view of the context. 駝 means "camel." So 放駝戶 means "camel herders." Therefore,

Fuchs is correct.

141. MS. 7a, line 8 has 愛興易. Fuchs, p. 466 corrects 愛興易 to 愛交易. In view of the context, 愛交易 makes sense.

142. After the Arab conquest the greater part of Persia was divided into four provinces: Khuzistan and Fars, attached to Basra; Media or Persian Iraq, attached to Kufa; Khursan; and Seistan. Relations between the Arab administration and the federal classes seem to have been generally good and a contingent of Iranian troops assisted Arabs in the conquests in Transoxiana (705–715) and repelling the later counter–attacks of the Central Asian Turks. There is abundant evidence that the Arabs intermarried extensively with the Iranian population. Abu Muslim took advantage of the tribal feuds by which the Arabs in Khurasan were divided; and adding his weight to a general rising of the Yemenite faction, he drove the Cmayyad governor out in 750, See *Encyclopedia Britannica,* Volume 17, p. 569.

143. MS. 7a, line 11 has 住不 but Fuchs, p. 466 has "不住." We follow Fuchs because 不住 is the correct order.

144. Fuchs, p. 450, note 8: "Mit Klein Fu–lin muss hier das Oströsjsche Syrien gemeint sein (Schaeder, p. 64). Die Bemerkung: und halt sich dort auf bezient sich auf die Vertegung der arabischen Haupstadt von Mekka nach Damaskus. Mit dem Ausdruck; in die Berge hineingehend ist offenbar der Taurus gemeint." *Encyclopedia Britanmica,* Volume 21, p.718:" Damascus was the capital of an Arab empire which extended by 715 from Spain and Morocco to Turkestan and Sind and held the mastery of the Mediterranean. With the wealth drawn from the dependent provinces the caliphs Abd ul–malik and Walid I endowed Jerusalem and Damascus with magnificent monuments. The first serious set back was the failure of the third and final Arab assault on Constantinople in 719."

145. MS, 7a, line 13 has 彼々國々. Fuchs, p. 466 divides 彼國 and 彼國. In view of the context, Fuchs' correction is right.

146. Fuchs, p 466 corrects 極窂 to 極窄. MS. 7a, line 12 has 極窂. 窂 means 'very tight' or 'cage'. 窄 means 'very narrow'. So Fuchs' correotion is right.

147. Fuchs, p. 466 has 女人在髮 but MS, 7b, line 1 has 人女在髮 Because 女人在髮 is the correct order, follow Fuchs.

148. [Ed.] MS, 7b, line 2 has 手把亦匙筯 But Fuchs, p. 466 corrects 手把亦匙筯 to 手把亦匙箸. 筯 means "sinew." Sadakata notes, "筯 is a popular character (俗字) of 箸 i. e. chopsticks. We feel, however, 'skewers' would be be more appropriate than chopsticks in that part of the world."

149. Fuchs, p. 451, note 2: "D. i. has Oströmisohe Reich mit Byzans." This is the Eastern Roman Emipire. According to Hye Ch'o s record, clothing of Eastern Romans Arabs, and Persians seemed to be similar. See 20,000 *Years of Fashion,* p. 345, and *History of Costume,* p. 119.

150. According to *Indosi and Chuoaziasi* 印度史中央亞細亞史 *(Indian and Central Asian History)* pp. 22, 74, 78, 95, and 65, An 安國 is Bukhari, Ts'ao 曹國 is Kaputana, Shih 史國 is Kashana, Shi–lo 石䃘國 is Shash which is today's Tashkent, Mi 米國 is Maimarg, and K'an 康國 is Samarkand. However, *Haneda Anniversary,* Vol. I, p. 401: "康國 is today's Tashkurgen." Cf. Fuchs, p. 451, note 4.

151. According to *Indosi and Chuoaziasi* p. 95 and 129, West–Tu–kuh exerted pressure on Ferghana. Also, in order to accomplish its complete conquest they attacked Kashgar and disturbed the border of T'ang (China). According to *National Geographic Magazine,* December, 1959, Atlas Plate 44, Ferghana is located between Tadzhik S. S. R. and Kirgiz S. S. R. Fuchs, p. 452, note 4: YHD liest ungenau 舵, T. T. richtig 那(二舥)."

152. Fuchs, p. 467 corrects 縛又大河 to 縛叉大河. This is in Russian territory today. Fuchs, p. 452, note 5: "So im Text. Lies 叉; dies bezeichnet eigentlich den Amu Darya; hier muss aber der Dir Darya gemeint sein; vgl. Shiratori, p. 137."

153. MS, 1 8a, line 9 has 男女剪髮. Fuchs, p. 467 corrects 男女剪髮 to 男人剪髮. Since later 女人在髮 appears, 男人 is correct.

153. Fuchs, p. 467, note 3: "已北 pleonastisch." Fuchs, p. 463, note 3: "MS liest hier pleonastisch: 至漢國已北." In view of the context, Fuchs' correction is right. This area would be from the Caspian sea to the Aral sea, or from the Aral sea to Balkhash.

155. [Ed.] MS, 8a, line 10 the character 宍 can faintly be seen. Fuchs, p. 453, note 4: "Dies Zeichen ist im MS undertlich verbessert; T. T. und YHD lesen 虫, Würmer, Hadani schlägt in seiner Einleitung 宍, eine alte Form für 肉, vor," Cf. *Haneda Anniversary,* Vol. I, p. 629, note 32: "宍 in Fuchs may be 虫. In other words it is 肉食." In agreement with Sadakata, however, we take it as 'insects (?)'.

156. MS, 8a, line 11. has 女人在頭. Fuchs, p. 468 corrects 女人在頭 to 女人在頭髮. Because 女人在頭 does not make sense and in view of the context, 女人在頭髮 makes sense.

157. Fuchs, p. 453, note 6: "Vgl. Doc., p. 164; Song Yun, p. 401." *Teihon sekai rekishi,* p. 38–39: "Wakkan is in Persia."

158. [Ed.] MS, 8b, line 1 has 偏樑難 but Fuchs, p. 468 has 難偏樑. In addition, Fuchs, p. 454, note I: "MS liest 樑, nicht 雖, wie die Textausgaben vorschlagen. 難 ist im MS klein nachgetragen und versehentlich hinter 樑 gesetzt anstatt hinter, 去." Either way, We take the meaning to be," "People are in danger walking on slanting bridges."

159. Fuchs, p. 468 has 江河浚崖醬, but MS. 8b, line 3, has 江河淩山至嚁.

160. [Ed.] Fuchs, p. 454 translates 龍門 as 'flowing course', but this should be read as 'the Dragon Gate water fall (in China)'.

161. MS, 8b, line 3 has 火上胲. Fuchs, p. 468 corrects 火上胲歌 to 火上陔

or 胲 or 垓. Fuchs, p. 454, note 4: "MS liest 上胲歌. Kai oder 胲 ist wohl 陔 oder 陔. Vieleicht ist 胲歌 hier, parallelzum nächsten Vers, als Gebirganame (unindentifiziert) aufzufassen."

162. [Ed.] MS, 8b, line 8 has 樹水. Fuchs, p. 468 corrects 樹水 to 樹木. Also Fuchs, p. 454. note 6: "MS liest 樹水, offenbar falsch fur 木." 樹木 means "tree water." 樹水 means "woods or trees." We, however, take this to mean 'tree' and 'water'.

163. Shignan or Shughnān in Badakhshanskaya, U. S. S. R. today, It is North west of Gilgit, Kashmir: 尸棄尼 in Hsüan-tsang's *Records*. Cf. Mizutani, *Daitō-Saiikkiki,* p. 381.

164–165. Since Hsüan-tsang did not actually go to Shignan, Hye Ch'o's descriptions are very valuable here.

166. 大播密川

167. 朅盤陀國 in Hsüan-tsang's *Records*. Tashkurghan (75° 10′ E., 37° 45′ N.) of today. Cf. Mizutani, ibid. p. 384.

168. According to Fujita, King P'ei–hsing s ancestral home was Kashgar. Cf. 唐書. 疏勒傳「王姓裴氏」or「喝盤陀其王本疏人世相承爲之」

169. *Kharbanda (Iran. *Yarpand or 'mountain way). Cf. Mizutani, ibid. p. 384.

170. Hsüan-tsang took same route on his way back to China.

171. 佉沙 in Hsüan-tsang's *Records.*

172. As for the etymology of Kashgar, there are two: Iran. *Kāsh* 'jewel' and *ghar* 'city', or Wakhān. *ghar* or 'mountains'. Cf. Mizutani, ibid. p. 389.

173. 守捉

174. MS. 9a, lines 8–9. 食肉及葱韮等也.

175. *Haneda Anniversary,* Vol. I, p. 507: 龜玆于闐 were Aryans and used the Kucha 龜玆 and Khotan 于闐 languages for everyday speech. According to *Kudangsue Sue-ik-jun* 舊唐書西域傳 (p. 116) and *Indosi and Chuoaziasi* 印度史中央亞細亞 (p. 20, 21, and 42) 30,000 Chinese troops were stationed in Kucha. The site of the General Protectorate of An–hsi 安西都護府 was placed here. In Kucha the Tokhāristān language was used among the people of Tarim basin at Kucha and Karashr, which are a part of Sin–kiang 新疆 (in China); this language is Indo–European.

176. The site of the General Protectorate of An–hsi maintained control of all nations of the Tarim basin, monitered nations to the west of Tash–kurgen, and managed the control or traffic and trade. This 安西都護府 was established in 640 A. D. after destroying 高昌國. In 648 A. D. the site of the General Protectorate of An–hsi conquered Kucha and moved here. Soon after, when the 太宗 emperor died, there was a rebellion at west Tu–kuh (阿史那賀魯).

177. Khotan 闐干, along with Kucha and Kashgar, directly belonged

to the site of the General Protectorate of An–hsi. See *Indosi and Chuoaziasi* 印度史中央亞細亞史, p. 114, 115. According to *Indosi and Chuoaziasi,* Chinese officials were appointed, held court trials, and ran the civil administration. The Khotanese language is an Indo–European language.

178. Fuchs, p. 456 added "D. i. Zwischen dem 18 and 27 Dezember 727."

179. According to Dr. Yi Byung Do, 節度大使 is an army commander and governor. Fuchs, p. 456, note 4: "Zum Titel vgl. T'P. XXV, 1928, p. 286 seq. Mit Chao ist Chao I–cheng 頤貞 gemeint, der zweite Generalprotektor von An–hsi, vgl. Doc. 364, s. v.; das 一切經音義, Kap. 100, Ende schreinbt 頤 fur 頤. Chao war nicht, wie Huei–ch'ao berichtet, erster General protektor; dies war damals Yen Wang–huei 延王迴"

180. Fuchs, p. 456, note 5: "有雨所漢僧住持. Zu 住持 vgl. p. 457, Anm 3."

181. 都維那; Fuchs, p. 456: Karmadana. According to 佛學大辭典, p. 2512 it means," a chief official who administers temple works."

182. *Bulkyo sajun,* p. 694: "This is one of the three divisions of holy scriptures."

183. 上座 means "student priest. ' While in the temple, he sometimes does errands. Regarding this, Yi U–Sung said the above.

184. *Indosi and Chvoaziasi* 印度史中央亞細亞, p. 117: "At the time of 則天武后 Ta–yün temples were established in states such as Kachgar (Kashgar) and An–hsi."

185. Fuchs, p. 457, note 3: "大好住持; 住持 ist hier in originaler, verhaler Bedeutung genommen (Oda, p. 1227, 3: Ruhig in der Welt leben und an Buddhas Lehre festhalten); sonst bedeutet es auch: Oberpriester oder Gemeinde Eigentum; vgl. dazu Chavannes–Pelliot, Traite–Manicheen, J. As. 1912, p. 555[1], und Chavannes, T'. P. 1904, p. 370[8]; hier p. 440, Anml 9."

186. The existence of 龍興寺 can be seen in 高昌 and 北庭(庭州). See p. 117 of *Indosi and Chuoaziasi* 印度史中央亞細亞史

187. Fuchs, p. 457, note 7: "MS unklar; wohl so zu lesen und nicht 烏, wie T. T. liest; vgl. Pelliot, T' P. XXXII, 1936, pp. 275–276."

188. According to *Indosi and Chvoaziasi,* p. 115 and *Tōyōgakuhō* 東洋學報, p. 103–6, Under the control of the site of the General Protectorate of An–hsi there were Kucha, Khotan, Kashgar, etc. where five characters are missing I added 安西都護府. In view of the context, this 安西都護府 is correct. According to *Indosi and Chuoaziasi* 印度史中央亞細亞史, p. 90, 安西都護府 depended on traffic–passing taxes from merchandizing Hu for the expense of ruling the four garrisons.

Part III

Manuscript and Edition

A Reproduction of the Manuscripts and Its Critical Edition*

The originals of the photographs of the manuscripts are in Paul Pelliot and Toyohachi Fujita, *Tonkō-isho Ei-in-hon Dai-isshū* (The Photographic Reproductions of Tun-huang Manuscripts 燉煌遺書, 影印本第一集), 1926, Shanghai, Tōakōkyūkai (東亜攷究会). The manuscripts were the acquisition of Paul Pelliot straight from a Tun-huang cave (Cf. BEFEO, 1908, pp.511–512). This discovery prompted the following works by a number of international scholars.

Walter Fuchs, "Huei-ch'ao's Pilgerreise durch Nordwest-Indien und Zentral Asien um 726." Sitzungsberichte der Preussisches Akademi der Wissenschaften Philologische-Historische Klasse, Dezember, 1938.

1. 羅振王「敦煌石室遺書」(第一册) 慧超往五天竺國傳殘卷札記 1909.
2. 藤田豊八「往五天竺國傳箋釋」1910, 北京
3. 藤田豊八「往五天竺國傳箋釋」校訂再版, 1911, 東京
4. 高楠順次郎編,「慧超往五天竺國傳箋釋, 慧超傳考」(大日本佛教遊方傳叢書第一) 1915.
5. パウル・ペリオ
   羽田 亨 共編「敦煌遺書」, 1926.
6. 大正大藏經, 五十四巻央傳部, 1927.
7. 藤田豊八「慧超往五天竺國傳箋釋」(錢稲孫印行), 1931. 北京
8. 大日本佛教全書 included Nos. 3 and 4, 1931.
9. 羽田亨「慧超往五天竺國傳迻錄」,「京都大學, 二千六百年央學論文集」, 1941.
10. 羽田亨 上記再錄「羽田博士央學論文集」上卷, pp.610–629.
11. 定方晟,‘「慧超往五天竺國傳」和釋’, 東海大學紀要文學部, 1971, pp.3–30.
12. 鈴木學術財團編 "慧超往五天竺國傳箋釋一卷" 藤田豊八編,
    (pp.299–325) :「慧超傳考」, 高楠順次郎編.
    (pp.326–335),「大日本佛教全書」, Vol. 73, 1972.

In the following editorial work, the different readings are noted on the basis of the works listed above. (Iida)

實赤足裸形外道亦著二
廷食肉葜亦不齋也地皆平
有奴婢將賣人罪与煞人罪不殊
一月至拘尸那國佛入涅槃處其城荒廢無人住也佛入涅槃處置塔有
禪師在彼掃灑每年八月八日僧尼道俗就彼大設供養於其空中有
幡現不知其數衆人同見當此之日發心非一此塔西有一河伊羅鉢底
水南流二千里外方入恒河彼塔四絕無人住也極荒林木往彼禮拜者被
犀牛大虫所損也此塔東南卅里有一寺名娑般檀寺有十集一十三五家
常供養彼禪師衣食令在塔所供養
日至彼羅痆斯國此國亦廢無王即六
彼五俱輪見素形像在於塔中
上有師子彼幢極麁五人合抱文里細
塔時并造此幢寺名達磨斫葛羅僧
外道不著衣服身上塗灰事於大天此寺中有一金銅像五百
乞摩揭陀國舊有一王名尸羅粟底造此像也兼造一金銅

1 （上缺）（1吠舍釐？）寶。赤足裸形外道不著衣（約十六字缺）
2 逢*食卽喫 亦不齋也。地皆平（約十六字缺）
3 有奴婢。將賣人罪与煞人罪不殊（約十五字缺）
4 （2拘尸那國）一月*至拘尸那國。仏入涅槃處。其城荒廢。無人住也。仏入涅槃處置塔。有
5 禪師在彼掃灑。每年八月八日。僧尼道俗。就*彼大設供養。於其空中有
6 幡現。不知其數。衆人同見。當此日ˇ之發心非一。此塔西有一河。伊羅鉢底。
7 水南流二千里外方入洹*河。彼塔四絕無人往**也。極荒林木。往彼礼拜者。□
8 犀牛大虫所損也。此塔東南卅里。有一寺。名娑*般檀寺。有卅**餘之村***庄三五所
9 常供養彼禪師衣食令在塔所供養（約十一字缺）
10 （3娑羅痆斯國）日。至彼羅痆斯國。此國亦廢無王郎*□（約十四字缺）（3）（5）麗）。
11 彼五俱輪。見素形像在於塔中（約十四字缺）
12 上有師子。彼幢極麁*五人合抱。文里細（約十三字缺）
13 塔時。并造此幢。寺名達磨斫葛羅僧（約十二字缺）
14 外道不著衣服。身上塗灰事於大天。此寺中有一金銅像。五百□□□。
15 是摩揭陁國舊有一王名尸羅粟*底。造此像也。兼造一金銅□□

2. *Ms 辻 F(ujita) or S(adkata) 逢

4. *Ms. 月 F. 日 H(aneda) 月

5. *Ms. 就 F. 乾 H. 就

7. *Ms 恒 S. 洹 H. 恒
**Ms. 往 F. 住

8. *Ms 妄 F. □ S. 娑 H. 娑
**Ms ?† F†S. 卅
***F. □□□□□□
S. 卅餘之村庄三五所
H. 州餘□村庄三五時

10. *Ms. 郎 F. □

12. *Ms. 麁 F. 麗

15. *Ms. 要 H. 票

輻圓圓匠寸卅餘步此城濱臨恒河北岸置也即此鹿野苑拘尸那
舍城摩訶菩提等四大靈塔在摩揭陀國王界此國大小乘俱行于
時得達摩訶菩提寺稱其本願非常歡喜略題述其愚志　五言
不慮菩提遠焉將鹿苑遙只愁懸路險非意業風飄八塔難誠見
參著經劫燒何其人願滿目覩在今朝　又即從此彼羅痆斯國西
月至中天竺國王住城名葛那及自此中天王境界極寬百姓繁鬧
王有九百頭象餘大首領各有三二百頭其王每自領兵馬鬪戰常與餘
天戰也天中王常勝彼國法自知象少兵少即請和每年輸稅不交陣相
殺也衣著言音人風法用五天相似唯南天村草百姓語有差別仕
宦之類中天不殊五天國法無有枷棒牢獄有罪之者據輕重罰錢亦無
刑戮上至國王下及黎庶不見遊獵放鷹走犬等事道路雖即足賊
取物即放亦不殤煞如若悋物即有損也土地甚暖百卉恒青無有霜

輻圓圓正等*卅餘步。**此城俯臨恒河北岸置也。即此鹿野苑。拘尸那舍城。摩訶菩提等四大靈塔。在摩揭陁國王界。此國大小乘俱行。□*□得達摩訶菩提寺。稱其本願。非常歡喜。略題述其愚志。五言不*慮菩提遠。焉將鹿苑遙。只愁懸路險。非意業風飄。八塔難誠見。參者經劫燒。何其人願滿。目覩在今朝。又即從此彼羅痆斯國西行*

*〔天、此寺中有一金銅像、五百□□□
栗底、造此像也、兼造一金銅□□〕

4 中天竺

□月。至中天竺國王住城。名葛那及自。此中天王境界極寬。百姓繁閙。王有九百頭象。餘大首領各有三二百頭。其王每自領兵馬鬪戰。常与餘四*天戰也。天〻中王常勝。彼國法。自知象少兵少。即請和。每年輸稅。不交陣相煞也。衣著言音。人風法用。五天相似。唯南天村草百姓。語有*差別。仕□之類。中天不殊。五天國法。爲有枷棒牢獄。有罪之者。據輕重罰錢。亦無刑戮。上至國王。下級黎庶。不見遊獵放鷹走犬等事。道路雖*即有足賊取物即放。亦不殤煞。*如若**惜物。即有損也。土地甚暖。百卉恒青。無有霜

(2)懷(3)↑(5)情

*〔天…銅□□〕 belongs to 1a, lines 14 and 15.

1. *Ms. 寸 F. 寸 S. 等 H. 等
   **Ms. 步 F. 卅餘當 H. 步

2. *F. 不

4. *Ms. 不 F. □ H. 不

5. *F.□□ S. 西行 H. □

7. *Ms.四 F. □ H. 四

9. *Ms.有 F. □ H. 有

11. *雖郎有足賊 F. 雖有足賊 H. 郎足賤

12. *Ms. 煞 F. 煞也. H. 煞
    **Ms. 如若惜(?)物 F.若↑物. H. 如若怯物

番食唯粳糧餅麨蘇乳酪等无醬有塩揔用土鍋煮飯而食
无鐵釜等也百姓无別庸税但抽田子五石与王〃自遣人運將田主亦
不為送也彼土百姓貧多富少王官屋裏及富有者着㲲一雙自餘
一隻貧者半片女人亦然其王每坐衙處首領百姓揔來遶王四面而坐各
諍道理訴訟紛紜非常亂鬧王聽不嗔緩〃報云汝是〃汝不是彼百
姓等取王一口語為定更不再言其王首領等甚敬信三寶若對師
僧前王及首領等在地而坐不肯坐床王及首領行坐來去處自
將牀子隨身到處即坐他牀不坐寺及王宅並皆三重作樓從下第
一重作庫上二重人住諸大首領等亦然屋皆平頭塼木所造自外
並皆草屋似於漢屋兩下作也又是一重土地所出唯有㲲布象馬等
物當土不出金銀並從外國來也亦不養駝騾驢猪等畜其牛總白
万頭之內希有一頭赤黑之者羊馬全少唯王有二三百口六七十疋自外
首領百姓揔不養畜唯愛養牛取乳酪蘇也土地人善不多相殺
於市店間不見有屠行賣肉之處此中天大小乘俱行即此中天界內有四

雪。食*唯粳粮餅麨蘇乳酪等。無醬有鹽。惣用土鍋炙飰而食。無鐵釜等也。百姓無別庸稅。但抽田子五一*石与王。々自遣人運將。田主□**不爲送也。彼土百姓。貧多富少。王官屋裏。及富有者。著氎一隻。自□一雙。貧者半片。女人亦然。其王每衙處首領百姓。惣*來遶王四面而坐。各諍道理。訴訟紛紜。非常亂閙王聽不嗔。緩々報云。汝是汝不是。彼百姓等。取王一口語爲定 更不再言 其王首領等。甚*敬信三寶。若對師僧前。王及首領等。在地而坐不肯坐床。王及首領。行坐來去處。自將床子隨身。到處即座。他床不坐。寺及王宅。並*皆三重作樓。從下第一重作庫。上二重人住。諸大首領等亦然。屋皆平頭。塼木所造。自外□並*皆草屋。似於漢**屋兩***下作也。又是一重。土地所出。唯有氎布象馬等****物。當土不出金銀。並*從外國來也。亦不養駝騾驢猪**等畜。其牛惣白。万頭之內。希有一頭赤黑之者。羊馬全少。唯王有三二*百口六七十疋。自外首領百姓。惣不養畜。唯愛養牛。取乳酪蘇也。土地人善。不多愛煞。於*市店間。不見有屠行賣肉之處〔**5 中天竺・四大塔**〕此中天大小乘俱行。即此中天界內有四

1. *Ms. 食. F. 雪。唾 粳粮.

2. *Ms. F.五石
**Ms. □ F. 田主 不鳥
H. 田主勞

4. *Ms. 惣. F. 總
H. 惣

6. *Ms. 甚. F. 其
H. 甚

8. *Ms. 並 F. 竝
H. 並

10. *Ms. 並. F. 竝
**Ms. 漢. F. 漢.
H. 漢
Fuchs. 漢.
***Ms. 雨下作.
Fujita 雨下作.
Fuchs. 雨下作.
S.兩下作.
****Ms. □ F. 萬.
S. 等

11. *Ms. 並. F. 竝.
H. 並
**Ms. 猪等 F. 諸 等 H. 猪等

12. *Ms. 三二. F. 二 三 H. 三二

14. *Ms. □ F. □ S. 於. H. 於.

大塔恒河在北岸有三大塔一舍衛國給孤薗中見有寺有僧二毗
耶離城菴羅薗中有塔見在其寺荒廢無僧　三迦毗耶羅國即仏本
生城無憂樹見在彼城已廢有塔無僧亦無百姓此城最居北林木荒
多道路足賊往彼礼拜者甚難方迷四三道寶階塔在中天王住城
西七日程在兩恒河間仏當從刀利天變成三道寶階下閻浮提地處左
金右銀中吠瑠璃仏於中道梵王左路帝釋右階侍仏下來即於此處
置塔見有寺有僧
即從中天國南行三箇餘月至南天竺國王所
住王有八百頭象境土極寬南至南海東至東海西至西海北至中天西
東天等國接界衣著飲食人風与中天相似唯言音稍別土地熱於
中天土地所出氎布象水牛黃牛亦少有羊無駝騾驢等有稻田無
黍粟等至於綿絹之屬五天總無王及領首百姓等極敬三寶足寺
足僧大小乘俱行於彼山中有一大寺是龍樹菩薩便夜叉神造非人

大塔。恆河在北岸有三大塔。一舎衞國給孤薗中。見有寺有僧。二。毘耶離城菴羅薗中。有塔見在。其寺荒廢無僧。三。迦毘耶羅國。卽仏本生城。無憂樹見在。彼城已廢。有塔無僧。亦無百姓。此城最居北*。林木荒多。道路足賊。往彼礼拜者。甚難方迷*。四。三道寶階塔。在中天王住城西七日程。在兩恆河間。仏當從刀利天變成三道寶階。下閻浮提地處。左金右金。中吠瑠璃。仏於中道。梵王左路。帝釋右階。侍仏下來。卽於此處置塔。見有寺僧*ㇾ有。〔6 **南天竺**〕 **卽從中天國南行三箇餘月。至南大竺國王所住。王有八百頭象。境土極寬。南至南海。東至東海。西至西海。北至中天。西天東天等國接界。衣著飲食人風。与中天相似。唯言音稍別。土地熱於中天。土地所出。氎布象水牛黃牛。亦少有羊。無駞騾驢等。有稻田。無黍粟等。至於綿絹之屬。五天惣*無。王及領ㇾ首百姓等**。極敬三寶。足寺足僧。大小乘俱行。於彼山中。有一大寺。是龍樹菩薩便*夜叉神造。非人

3. *Ms. 比. F. 比或北之譌 H. 比

4. *Ms. 迷 F. 迷殆途之譌 H. 迷

7. *Ms. 僧有. H. 僧有

**F. 此上原空二字. The space could well be, however, the indication of the new chapter.

11. *Ms. 惣. F. 總
**Ms. 等. F. 百姓. H. 等

12. *Ms. 便. F. 羅君札記云. 便當作使. H. 便

所作並鑿山為柱三重作樓四面方圓三百餘步龍樹在日寺有三千
僧獨供養以十五石米每日供三千僧其米不竭取却還生元不減少
然今此寺廢無僧也龍樹壽年七百方始亡也于時在南天路為言曰
言　月夜瞻鄉路浮雲颯颯歸緘書忝去便風急不聽迴我國
岸北他邦地角西日南無有鴈誰為向林飛
又從南天北行兩月至西天國王住城此西天王亦五六百頭象土地所出氎
布及銀象馬羊牛多出大小二麥及諸豆等稻穀全少食多餅麨
乳酪蘇油市買用銀錢氎布之屬王及首領百姓等極敬信三寶足
寺足僧大小乘俱行土地甚寬西至西海國人多善唱歌餘四天國不
如此國又無枷棒牢獄刑戮等事見今被大寔來侵半國已損又五天
法出外去者不將糧食到處即便乞得食也唯王首領等出自齎
糧不食百姓祗擬　又從西天北行三箇餘月至北天國也名闍

所作。並*鑿山爲柱。三重作樓。四面方圓三百餘步。龍樹在日。寺有三千僧。獨供養以十五石米。每日供三千僧。其米不竭。取却還生。元不減少。然今此寺廢。無僧也。龍樹壽年七百。方始亡也。于時在南天路。爲言曰。五言　月夜瞻*鄉路。浮雲颱〻歸。減**書參去便。風急不聽迴。我國天岸北。他邦地角西。日南無有鴈。誰爲向林*飛。〔7　**西天竺**〕又從南天北行兩月。至西天國王住城。此西天王亦五六百頭象。土地所出氎布及銀象馬羊牛。多出大小二麥及諸荳等。稻穀全少。食多餅麨乳酪蘇油。市買用銀錢氎布之屬。王及首領百姓等。極敬信三寶。足寺足僧。大小乘俱行。土地甚寬。西至西海。國人多善唱歌。餘四天國不如此國。又無枷棒牢獄形戮等事。見今被大寔來侵半國已損。又五天法。出外去者。不將粮*食。到處即便乞得食也。唯王首領等出。自齎糗*不食百姓**[illegible]〔8　**北天竺、闍蘭達羅國**〕又從西天北行三箇餘月。至北天國也。名闍

1. *Ms. 並. F. 竝.

4. *Ms. 瞻鄉. F. □□ or 瞻那. H. 瞻鄉
**Ms. 減. F. 緘
H. 緘

5. *Ms. 林. F. 牀
H. 林

11. *Ms. 粮. F. 糧.
H. 粮

12. *Ms. 粮. F. 糧.
**Ms. ネ？米？
S. 祇從. F. □□
H.

蘭達羅國王有三百頭象依山作城而住從茲已北漸々有山為國
狹小兵馬不多常被中天及迦葉彌羅國屢々所吞所以依山而住人
風衣著言音与中天不殊土地稍冷於中天等也无霜雪但有風
冷土地所出象氎布稻麥驢騾少有其王有馬百疋首領三五疋百
姓並无西是平川東近雪山國內足寺足僧大小乘俱行又一月程過雪
山東有一小國名蘇跋那具怛羅屬土蕃國所管衣著与北天相似言
音即別土地極寒也又從此闍蘭達羅國西行經一月至一社吒國言
音稍別大分相似衣著人風土地所出節氣寒暖与北天相似亦足寺足僧
大小乘俱行王及首領百姓等大敬信三寶　又從此吒國西行一月至新頭故羅
國衣著風俗節氣寒暖与北天相似言音稍別此國極足駱駝國人取乳
酪喫也王及百姓等大敬三寶足寺足僧即造順正理論衆賢論師
是此國人也此國大小乘俱行見今大寔侵半國損也即從此國乃至五
天不多飲酒遍歷五天不見有醉人相打之者縱有飲者得色得力

蘭達羅國。王有三百頭象。依山作城而住。從玆已北。漸々有山。爲國狹小兵馬不多。常被中天及迦葉弥羅國屢々所呑。所以依山而住。人風衣著言音。与中天不殊。土地稍冷於中天等也。亦無霜雪。但有風冷。土地所有出家氍布稻麦驢騾少有。其王有馬百疋。首領三五疋。百姓並*無。西是平川。東近雪山。國內足寺足僧。大小乘俱行。(9 **蘇跋那具怛羅**) 又一月程過雪山。東有一小國。名蘇跋那具怛羅。屬土蕃*國所管。衣著□**北天相似。言音即別。土地極寒也。(10 **社吒國**) 又從此闍蘭達羅國西行。經一月。至一社吒國。言音稍別。大分相似。衣著人風。土地所出。節氣寒暖。与北天相似。亦足寺足僧。大小乘俱行。王及首領百姓等。大敬三寶。(11 **新頭故羅國**) 又從此吒國西行一月。至新頭故羅國。衣著風俗。節氣寒暖。与北天相似。言音稍別。此國極足駱駝。國人取乳酪喫也。王及百姓等、大敬三寶。足寺足僧。即造順正理論。衆賢論師。是此國人也。此國大小乘俱行。見今大寔侵*半國損也。即從此國乃至五天。不多飲酒。遍歷五天。不見有醉人相打之者。縱有飲者。得色*力

5. *Ms. 並. F. 竝. H. 並

6. *Ms. 蕃. F. 番. H. 蕃

**Ms. ?. F. 輿. H. 與

†2. *Ms. ?. F. 侵. H. 侵

13. *Ms. 色. F. 氣 H. 色

而王不見有歌舞作劇飲宴之者　又從北天國有一寺名多摩三
磨娑仏在之日来此說法廣度人天此寺東澗裏於泉水邊有一塔而
仏所剃頭及剪爪甲在此塔中此見有三百餘僧寺有大辟支仏牙及
骨舍利等更有七八所寺各五六百人大好住持王及百姓等非常敬信
又山中有一寺名那揭羅馱娜有一漢僧於此寺身亡彼大德說從中天来明
閑三藏聖教將欲還鄉忽然違和便即化矣于時聞說莫不傷心便題四
韻以悲冥路　五言　故里燈無主他方寶樹摧神靈去何處玉皃已成灰
憶想哀情切悲君願不隨孰知鄉國路空見白雲歸
又從此北行十五日入山至迦羅國此迦羅亦是北天數此國稍大王有三百
頭象住在山中道路險惡不被外國所侵人民繁多貧多富少王及首領
諸富有者衣著與中天不殊自外百姓悉被毛毯覆其形醜土地出銅鐵氈
布毛毯牛羊有象少馬粳米蒲桃之類土地極寒不同已前諸國秋霜
冬雪夏足霖雨百卉亟青葉彫冬草悉枯川谷狹小南北五日程東西一

而已。不見有歌儛*作劇飲宴之者。〔12 **多摩三磨娜寺**〕又從北天國有一寺。名多摩三磨娜。仏在之日。來此說法。廣度人天。此寺東澗裏。於泉水邊有一塔。而仏所剃頭又剪爪甲。在此塔中。此見有三百餘僧。寺有大*辟支佛牙及骨舍利等。更有七八所寺。各五六百人。大好住持。王及百姓等。非常敬信。

〔13 **郍揭羅馱娜寺**〕又山中有一寺。名郍*揭羅馱娜。有一漢僧。於此寺身亡。彼大德說。從中天來。明閑三歲聖教將欲還鄉。忽然違*和。便卽化矣。于時聞說。莫不傷心。便題四韻。以悲冥路。五言 。故里燈無主。他方寶樹摧。神靈去何處。玉皃已成灰。憶想哀情切。悲君願不隨。孰知鄉國路。空見白雲歸

〔14 **迦濕彌羅**〕又從此北行十五日。入山至迦羅國。此迦彌羅。亦是北天數*。此國稍大。王有三百頭象。住在山中。道路險惡。不被外國所侵*。人民極衆。貧多富少。王及首領諸富有者。衣著與中天不殊。自外百姓。悉支*毛毯。覆其形醜。土地出銅鐵氎布毛毯牛羊。有象少馬粳米蒲桃之類。土地極寒。不同已前諸國。秋霜多雪。夏足霖*雨百卉亙青。葉稠**多草悉枯。川谷狹小。南北五日程。東西一

1. *Ms. 儛. F. 舞 H. 儛

3. *Ms. 火. F.火. S. 大 H. 大

5. *Ms. 郍. F. 那. H. 那

6. *Ms. 逺. F. 羅君札記日逺乃違之別字.

9. *Ms. 北天數. F. 北數. H. 北數逺

10. *Ms. . F. 侵. H. 侵

11. *Ms. 枝. F. 羅君札記日. 枝殆被之譌 Fuchs.支. H.

13. *Ms. 雲. F. 霜, 羅君札記云. 霜字疑誤. Fuchs. 霖.

**Ms. 彫. Fuchs. 稠. F. 羅君札記云 … 青葉彫此句有誤字. H. 彫

日行土地即盡餘並陰山屋並板木覆亦不用草瓦王及首領百姓等
甚敬三寶國內有一龍池彼龍王每日供養不一羅漢僧雖無人見彼聖
僧食亦過齋已即見餅飯從水下紛紛亂上以此得知迄今供養不絕王及大
首領出外乘象小官乘馬百姓並皆途步國內足寺足僧大小乘俱行五
天國法上至國王王妃王子下至首領及妻隨其力能各自造寺
也還別作不共修營彼云各自功德何須共造此既如然餘王子等亦爾
凡造寺供養即施村莊百姓供養三寶無有空造寺不施百姓者為
外國法王及妃姤各別村莊百姓王子首領各有百姓布施自由不王也造寺亦然
須造即造不問王王亦不敢遮怕招罪也若富有百姓雖無村莊布施亦勵
力造寺以自經紀得物供養三寶為五天不賣人無有奴婢要須布
施百姓村薗也　又迦葉彌羅國東北隔山十五日程即是大勃律國楊
同國娑播慈國此三國並屬吐蕃所管衣着言音人風並別著皮
裘氎衫靴褲等也地狹小山川極險亦有寺有僧敬信三寶若是

日行。土地卽盡。餘並*蔭山。屋並*板木覆上不用草瓦。王及首領百姓等。甚敬三寶。國內有一龍池。彼龍王每日供養千*一羅漢僧。雖無人見彼聖僧食。亦過齋巳。卽見餠飯從水下紛紛亂上。以此得知。迄今供養不絕。王及大首領出外乘象。小官乘馬。百姓並*皆途**步。國內足寺足僧。大小乘俱行。五天國法。上至國王。*至國王王妃王子。下至首領及妻隨其力能各自造寺也。還別作。不共修營。彼云。各自功德。何須共造。此旣如然。餘王子等亦尒。凡造寺供養。卽施村庄百姓供養三寶。無有空造寺不施百姓者。爲外國法。王及妃姤*。各別村庄百姓。王子首領。各有百姓。布施自由不**王也。造寺亦然。須造卽造。亦不問王。〻亦不敢遮。怕佔*罪也。若富有百姓。雖無村庄布施。亦勵力造寺。以自經紀。得物供養三寶。爲五天不賣人。無有奴婢。要須布施百姓村薗也。(15 **大勃律國、揚同國、娑播慈國**) 又迦葉彌羅國東北。隔山十五日程。卽是大勃律國揚同國。娑播慈國。此三國並屬吐蕃所管。衣著言音人風並*別。著皮裘氎衫靴袴等也。地狹小。山川極險。亦有寺有僧。敬信三寶。若是

1. *Ms. 並. F. 竝, H. 並

2. *Ms. 不; F. 不; S. 千. H. 一千

4. *Ms. 並. F. 竝. H. 並
**Ms. 途. F. 案途殆徒之誤. H. 途

5. Fuchs wrongly emends to: 至國王妃王子. H. 國王王妃

8. *Ms. 姤. Fuchs wrongly emends to: 后. H.
**Ms. 不王也不問王也, rightly changes to 不王 H. 不王也

9. *Ms. 拈. Fuchs.佔. H. 拈

已東吐蕃惣無寺舍不識仏法當土是胡所以信也已東吐蕃國純住氷
山雪山川谷之間　以氈帳而居無有城郭屋舍處所与突厥相似隨
逐水草其王雖在一處無有城但依氈帳以為居業土地出羊馬猫牛
毯褐之類衣著毛褐皮裘女人亦尓土地極寒不同餘國家常食麨
少有餅飯國王百姓等惣不識仏法無有寺舍國人悉皆穿地作坑而
臥無有床席人民極黑白者全希言音与諸國不同多愛喫虱為著毛
褐甚饒蟣虱捉得便抛口裏終不弃也　又迦葉弥羅國西北隔山七日
程至小勃律國此屬漢國所管衣著人風飲食言音与大勃律相似著
氎衫及靴剪其鬚髮頭上纏疊布一條女人在髮貧多富少山川狹
田種不多其山憔杌元無樹木及於諸草其大勃律元是小勃律王所住
之處為吐蕃來逼走入小勃律國坐首領百姓在彼大勃律不來
又從迦葉弥羅國西北隔山一月程至建馱羅此王及兵馬惣是突厥土人
胡兼有婆羅門此國舊是罽賓王王化為此突厥王阿耶領一部落兵馬投

巳東吐蕃。總無寺舍。不識佛法。當土是胡。所以信也。〔16 **吐蕃國**〕巳東吐蕃國。純住氷*山雪山川谷之間。以氈帳而居。無有城墎屋舍。處所與突厥相似。隨逐水草。其王雖在一處。亦無城。但依氈帳以爲居業。土地出羊馬猫牛毯褐之類。衣著毛褐皮裘。女人亦尓。土地極寒。不同餘國。家常食麨。少有餅飰。國王百姓等。惣不識佛法。無有寺舍。國人悉皆穿地作坑*而臥。無有床*席。人民極黑。白者全希**。言音與諸國不同。多愛喫虱。爲著毛褐。甚饒蟣虱。捉得便抛*口裏。終不弃也。〔17 **小勃律國**〕又迦葉彌羅國西北。隔山七日程。至*小勃律國。此屬漢國所管。衣著人風。飲食言音。與大勃律相似。著氎衫及靴剪其鬚髮頭上僫*疊布一條。女人在髮*、貧多富少。山川狹小。田種不多。其山憔杌*。元無樹木及於諸草。其大勃律。元是小勃律王所住之處。爲吐蕃*來逼。走入小勃律國坐。首領百姓。在彼大勃律不來。〔18 **建駄羅**〕又從迦葉彌羅國西北隔山一月程。至建駄羅。此王及兵馬。惣是突厥。土人是胡。兼有婆羅門。此國舊是罽賓王王化。爲此突厥王阿耶領一部落兵馬。投

1. *Ms. 氷. F. 冰. H. 氷

5. *Ms. 抗. F. 羅君札記云. 抗殆坑之譌. Fuchr, 坑. H. 杭

6. *Ms. 床. F. 牀. **Ms. 布. F. 希. Fuchs. 希. H. 床

7. *Ms. 杖. F. 羅君札記云. 杖郎抛之別字. H.

8. *Ms. ?. F. 在. S. 至. H. 至

9. *Ms. 僫. F. 纒. **MS. =髮. H. 纒

10. *Ms. . F. 杌. H. 杌

11. *Ms. 蕃. F. 番. H. 番

彼罽賓王於後突厥兵盛便煞彼罽賓王自為國主因茲國境突厥霸
此國已北並住中其山並燋無草及樹衣著人風言音節氣並別衣是皮毬
氈衫靴袴之類土地宜大麥小麥全無黍粟及稻人多食麨及餅唯除
迦葉彌羅大勃小勃楊同等國即此建馱羅國乃至五天崑崙等國總無蒲桃
甘蔗此突厥王象有五頭羊馬無數駝騾驢等甚多漢地興胡
迴不過向南為道路險惡多足劫賊從茲已北西業者多□
之間極多屠煞此王雖是突厥甚敬信三寶王王妃王子首領等各各造寺供
養三寶此王每年兩迴設無遮大齋但是緣身所受用之物妻及象馬等
並皆捨施唯妻及象令僧斷價王還自贖自餘駝馬金銀衣物家具聽僧
賣自分利養此王不同餘已北突厥也兒女亦然各各造寺設齋捨施此城俯臨辛頭
大河北岸而置此城西三日程有一大寺即是天親菩薩無著菩薩所住之寺此寺名葛
諾歌有一大塔每常放光此寺及塔舊時葛諾歌王造從王立寺名也又此城東南
里即是佛過去為尸毗王救鴿處見有寺有僧又佛過去捨頭捨眼餧五夜叉

彼罽賓王。於後突厥兵盛。便煞彼罽賓王。自爲國主。因玆國境突厥霸王此國已北。*並住中。其山*並燋無草及樹。衣著人風言音節氣*並別。衣是皮**毬氎衫靴袴之類土地宜大麥小麥。全無黍粟及稻。人多食麨及餅。唯除迦葉彌羅大勃小勃揚同等國。即此建馱羅國。乃至五天崑崙等國。*惣無蒲*桃唯有甘蔗。此突厥王象有五頭。羊馬無數。駞騾驢等**甚多漢地與胡*戰而不歸東廻不過。向南爲道路險惡。多足劫賊。從玆已北。惡**業者多。市店*之間。極多屠煞。此王雖是突厥。甚敬信三寶。王王妃王子首領等。各各造寺。供養三寶。此王每年兩廻設無遮大齋。但是緣身所*受用之物。妻及象馬等。*並皆捨施。唯妻及象。令僧斷價。王還自贖。自餘駞馬金銀衣物家具。聽僧貨賣。自分利養。此王不同餘已北突厥也。兒女亦然。各各造寺。設齋捨施。此城俯臨辛頭大河北岸而置。此城西三日程有一大寺。即是天親菩薩無着菩薩所住之寺。此寺名葛諸歌。有一大塔。每常放光。此寺及塔。舊時葛諸歌王造。從王立寺名也。又此城東南□里。即是佛過去爲尸毘王*救鴿處。見有寺有僧。又佛過去捨頭捨眼餧五夜叉

2. *Ms. 並. F. 竝. H. 並
**Ms. 毬. Fuchs. 毬. H. 毬

4. *Ms. 惣. F. 總.

5. *Ms.□□□ Fuchs. 桃唯有
**Ms. 甚漢多. F. 等甚多. Fuchs. 甚多漢地

6. *Ms. □□□□□.
**Ms. 西業. H. 西業

7. *Ms. 之間. F. □□.

8. H. 愛

9. *Ms. 並. F. 竝. H. 並

13. *Ms.救. F. 放. H. 救

等處並在此國中在此城東南山裏各有寺有僧見今供養此國大小乘俱行
又從此建馱羅國正北入山三日程至烏長國彼自云鬱地引那此王大敬三寶百姓村莊多
分施入寺家供養少分自留以供養衣食設齋供養每日是常足寺足僧僧稍多
於俗人也專行大乘法也衣著飲食人風與建馱羅國相似言音不同土地足駝騾
羊馬氎布之類節氣甚冷　又從烏長國東北入山十五日程至拘衛國
自呼云奢摩褐羅闍國此王亦敬信三寶有寺有僧衣著言音與烏長
國相似氈衫袴等亦有羊馬等也　又從此建馱羅國西行入山七日至覽波
國此國無王有大首領亦屬建馱羅國所管衣著言音與建馱羅國相似
亦有寺有僧敬信三寶行大乘法　又從此覽波國而行入山經於八日程至罽
賓國此國亦是建馱羅王所管此王夏在罽賓逐涼而坐冬往建馱羅趁暖
而住彼即無雪暖而不寒其罽賓國冬天積雪為此冷也此國土人是胡王及兵馬
突厥衣著言音食飲與吐火羅國大同少異無問男之與女並皆著氎布衫
袴及靴男女衣服無有差別男人並剪鬚髮女人髮在土地出駝騾羊馬驢牛

等處。並*在此國中。在此城東南山裏。** 各有寺有僧。見今供養。此國大小乘俱行。〔19 烏長國〕又從此建馱羅國。正北入山三日程。至烏長國。彼自云鬱地引舥。此王大敬三寶。百姓村荘。多分施入寺家供養。少分自留。以供養衣食。設齋供養每日是常。足寺足僧。ゝ稍多於俗人也。專行大乘法也。衣著飲食人風。與建馱羅國相似。言音不同。土地足駞騾羊馬氎布之類。節氣甚冷。〔20 拘衞國〕又從烏長國。東北入山十五日程。至拘衞國。彼自呼云奢摩褐羅闍國。此王亦敬信三寶。有寺有僧。衣著言音。與烏長國相似。著氎衫袴等。亦有羊馬等也。〔21 覽波國〕又從此建馱羅國。西行入山七日。至覽波*國。此國無王。有大首領。亦屬建馱羅國所管。衣著言音。與建馱羅國相似亦有寺有僧。敬信三寶。行大乘法。〔22 罽賓國〕又從此覽波*國而行入山。經於八日程。至罽賓國。此國亦是建馱羅王所管。此王夏在罽賓。逐涼而坐。多往建馱羅。趁*暖而住。彼卽無雪。暖而不寒。其罽賓國多天積雪。爲此冷也。此國土人是胡。王及兵馬突厥。衣著言音食飮。與吐火羅國。大同少異無問男之與女。並皆著氎布衫袴及靴。男女衣服無有差別。男人並*剪鬢髮。女人髮在。土地出駞騾羊馬驢牛

1. *Ms. 並. F. 竝.
**Ms. 東南山裏
F. 東南裏

7. *Ms. ?. F. 彼. S. 波. H. 波

9. *Ms. 波. F. 波.

10. *Ms. 趂. Fuchs. 趁 H. 趂

13. *Ms. 並. F. 竝.

氎布蒲桃大小二麦鬱金香等國人大敬信三寶足寺足僧百姓家各絲造寺
供養三寶大城中有一寺名沙糸寺寺中見佛螺髻骨舍利見在王官百姓每日供
養此國行小乘亦住山裏山頭無有草木恰似火燒山也　又從此罽賓國西行
至七日謝䫻國彼自呼云社護羅薩他那土人是胡王及兵馬即是突厥其
王即是罽賓王姪兒自把部落兵馬住於此國不屬餘國亦不屬阿叔此王
及首領雖是突厥極敬三寶足寺足僧行大乘法有一大突厥首領名娑
鐸幹每年一迴設金銀無數多於彼王衣著人風土地所出與罽賓王相似
言音各別　又從謝䫻國北行七日至犯引國此王是胡不屬餘國兵馬強
諸國不敢來侵衣著氎布衫皮毬氈衫等類土地出羊馬氎布之屬甚
足蒲桃土地有雪極寒住多依山王及首領百姓等大敬三寶足寺足僧
大小乘法此國及謝䫻等亦並剪鬚髮人風大分與罽賓相似別異處
多當土言音不同餘國　又從此犯引國北行廿日至吐火羅國王住城名為
縛底耶見今大寔兵馬在彼鎮押其王被逼走向東一月程在蒲特

1 氎布蒲桃大小二麥欝金香等。國人大敬信三寶。足寺足僧。百姓家各絲*造寺。

2 供養三寶。大城中有一寺。名沙糸寺。〻*中見佛螺髻骨舍利。見在王官百姓每日供

3 養。此國行小乘。亦住山裏。山頭無有草木。恰似火燒山也。〔23 **謝䫻國**〕又從此罽賓國西行

4 *至七日謝䫻國。彼自呼云社護羅薩他䎒。土人是胡。王及兵馬。郎**是突厥。其

5 王郎是罽賓王姪兒。自把部落兵馬住此*〻於國。不屬餘國。亦不屬阿狀**此王

6 及首領。雖是突厥。極敬三寶。足寺足僧。行大乘法。有一大突厥首領。名娑

7 鐸幹。每年一迴。設金銀無數。多於彼王。衣著人風。土地所出。與罽賓王相似。言

8 音各別。〔24 **犯引國**〕又從謝䫻國。北行七日。至犯引國。此王是胡。不屬餘國。兵馬强多。

9 諸國不敢來侵*。衣著氎布衫皮毬氎衫等類。土地出羊馬氎布之屬。甚

10 足蒲桃。土地有雪。極寒住多依山。王及首領百姓等。大敬三寶。足寺足僧。行

11 大小乘法。此國及謝䫻。亦並剪於鬢髮。人風大分與罽賓相似。別異處

12 多。當土言音。不同餘國。〔25 **吐火羅國**〕又從此犯引國。北行廿日。至吐火羅國。王住城名爲

13 縛底䎒。見今大寔兵馬。在彼鎭押。其王被逼*。走向東一月程。在蒲

1. *Ms. 絲；F. 羅君札記曰. 各絲或各自之譌 H. 竝

2. *Ms.貝？見？F. 貝, 羅君札記云貝殆有之譌. S. 見 H. 見

4. *Ms. 至；F. H. 西行七日至.
**Ms. H. 郎是；F. 但是

5. *F. 羅君札記. 此於二字倒置.
**Ms. 狀；F.H. 叔

9. *Ms. 侵. F.H. 侵.

13. *Ms. 其王被其王被逼 F. 羅君札記云. 下其王被三字衍.

特山住見屬大寔所管言音与諸國別共罽賓國少有相似多分不同衣
着皮毬氎布等上至國王下及黎庶皆以皮毬為上服土地足駝騾羊馬
氎布蒲桃食唯愛餅土地寒冷冬天霜雪也國王首領及百姓等甚敬三
寶足寺足僧行小乘法食肉及葱韮等不事外道男人並剪鬚髮女人在髮
土地足山　又從吐火羅國西行一月至波斯國此王先管大寔大寔是波斯王放駝
戶於後叛便煞彼王自立為主然今此國却被大寔所吞衣舊着寬氎布衫
剪鬚髮食唯餅肉縱然有米亦磨作餅喫也土地出駝騾羊馬出高大
驢氎布寶物言音各別不同餘國土地人性愛興易常於西海汎舶入南海
向師子國取諸寶物所以彼國云出寶物亦向崑崙國取金亦汎舶漢地直
至廣州取綾絹絲綿之類土地出好細疊國人愛煞生事天不識佛法
又從波斯國北行十日入山至大寔國彼王住不本國見向小拂臨國住也為
打得彼國彼國復居山島處所極牢為此就彼土地出駝騾羊馬疊布毛毯
亦有寶物衣着細疊寬衫衫上又披一疊布以為上服王及百姓衣服一種無別

1 特*山住。見屬大寔所管。言音与諸國別。共罽賓國少有相似。** 多分不同。衣
2 著皮毬氎布等。上至國王。下及黎庶。皆以皮毬。爲上服。土地足駝騾羊馬
3 氎布蒲桃。食唯愛餅。土地寒冷。多天霜雪也。國王首領及百姓等。甚敬三
4 寶。足寺足僧。行小乘法。食內*及葱韮**等。不事外道。男人並剪鬢髮。女人在髮。土
5 地足山。〔26 **波斯國**〕又從吐火羅國。西行一月。至波斯國。此王先管大大*。寔ゝ是波斯王放駝
6 戶。於後叛。便煞彼王。自立爲主。然今此國。却被大駝所呑。衣舊著寬氎布衫
7 剪鬢髮。食唯餅肉。縱然有米。亦磨作餅喫也。土地出駝氎羊馬。出高大
8 驢氎布寶物。言音各別。不同餘國。土地人性。愛*與易。常於西海汎舶。入南海。
9 向師子國。取諸寶物。所以彼國云出寶物。亦向崑崙國取金。亦汎舶漢地。直
10 至廣州。取綾絹絲綿之類。土地出好細疊。國人愛煞生。事天不識佛法。〔27 **大寔國**〕
11 又從波斯國。北行十日入山至大寔國。彼王住ゝ不本國。見向小拂臨國*住也。爲
12 打得彼ゝ*國ゝ復居山島。處所極窄。爲此就彼。土地出駝騾羊馬疊布毛毬
13 亦有寶物。衣著細疊寬衫。ゝ上又披一疊布。以爲上服王及百姓衣服。一種無別

1. *Ms. 特?, 持? F. 持; S.H. 特.
**Ms. 有. F. 爲

4. *Mr. 內. F; 羅君札記日. 案內殆肉之譌
**Ms. 葱悲. H. 食肉
F. 慈悲; 羅君札記日. 慈悲殆葱韮之譌

5. Ms. 先管大大寔;
F. 先管大寔.
H. 大

8. *Ms. 受夫易; F. 受夫易, 羅君札記云. 案受殆愛之譌. 夫殆交之譌 H. 愛興易

11. *Ms.. 國, F. 小拂臨住

12. *Ms. 彼: 國; F.爲打得彼國. 彼國復居山島 H. 彼國

女人亦着寬衣男人剪鬚髮在頭女人在髮喫食無問貴賤共同一盆而
食手把亦匙筋取見極惡云自手煞而食得福無量國人愛煞事天
不識仏法國法無有跪拜法也　又小拂臨國傍海西北即是大拂臨
國此王兵馬強多不屬餘國大寔數回討擊不得突厥侵亦不得土
地足寶物甚足駝騾羊馬疊布等物衣著與波斯大寔相似言
音各別不同　又從大寔國已東並是胡國即是安國曹國史國石騾
國米國康國中雖各有王並屬大寔所管為國狹小兵馬不多不能自
護土地出駝騾羊馬疊布之類衣著疊衫袴等及皮毬言音不同
諸國　又此六國總事火祆不識仏法唯康國有一寺有一僧又不解敬也
此等胡國並剪鬚髮愛著白氎帽子極惡風俗婚姻交雜納母及
姊妹為妻波斯國亦納母為妻其吐火羅國乃至罽賓國犯引國謝
䫻國等兄弟十人五人三人兩人共娶一妻不許各娶一婦恐破家計

女人亦著寬衫。男人剪髮在鬢。女人*在髮。喫食無問貴賤。共同一盆而食。手把亦匙筯*取。見極惡。云自手煞而食。得福無量。國人愛煞事天。不識仏法。國法無有跪拜法也。〔28 **大拂臨國**〕又小拂臨國。傍海西北。即是大拂臨國。此王兵馬强多。不屬餘國。大寔數迴討擊不得。突厥侵*亦不得。土地足寶物。甚足駞騾羊馬疊布等物。衣著与波斯大寔相似。言音各別不同。〔29 **安國、曹國、史國、石騾國、米國、康國**〕又從大寔國已東。並是胡國。即是安國。曹國。史國。石騾國。米國。康國等*。雖各有王並**屬大駞所管。爲國狹小。兵馬不多。不***能自護。土地出駞騾羊馬疊布之類。衣著疊衫袴等*及皮毬。言音不同諸國。又此六國惣*事火祇。不識仏法。唯康國有一寺。有一僧。又不解敬也。此等*胡國。並**剪鬢髮。愛著白氎帽子。極惡風俗。婚姻交雜。納母及姊妹爲妻。波斯國亦納母爲妻。其吐火羅國。乃至罽賓國。犯引國。謝颶國等*。兄弟十人五人三人兩人。共娶一妻。不許各娶一婦。恐破家計。

1. *Ms. 人女. F.H. 女人.
2. *Ms. 筯. F. 箸. H. 筯
4. *Ms. 侵. F.H. 侵.
7. *Ms. 中？, F. 中. **Ms. 並. F. 竝. ***Ms. 不？, 而？ F. 而能. H. 不能
8. *Ms. 等？ F. 帶. H. 等
9. *Ms. 惣. F. 總. H. 惣
10. *Ms. 等？, 中？, F. 中. H. 等 **Ms. 並, F. 竝.
12. *Ms. 等？, 中？, F. 中. H. 等

又從康國已東即跋賀那國有兩王縛又大河當中西流河南一王屬大
寔河北一王屬突厥所管土地亦出駝騾羊馬疊布之類衣著皮裘疊
布食多餅麨言音各別不同餘國不識仏法无有寺舍僧尼
又跋賀那國東有一國名骨咄國此王元是突厥種族當土百姓半胡半
突厥土地出駝騾羊馬牛驢蒲桃疊布毛毯之類衣著疊布皮裘
言音半吐火羅半突厥半當土王及首領百姓等敬信三寶有寺有僧行
小乘法此國屬大寔所管外國雖云道國共漢地一箇大州相似國男人
剪鬚髮女人在髮　又從此胡國已北北至北海西至西海東至漢國已
北總是突厥所住境界此等突厥不識仏法无寺无僧衣著皮毬
氈衫以虫為食亦無城郭住處氈帳為屋行住隨身隨逐水草
男人並剪鬚髮女人在頭言音与諸國不同國人愛煞不識善惡土地足駝騾
羊馬之屬　又從吐火羅國東行七日至胡蜜王住城當來於吐火羅國逢
漢使入蕃略題四韻取辞　五言　君恨西蕃遠余嗟東路長

〔30 **跋賀那國**〕又從康國已東 即跋賀舥國。有*兩王。縛又大河。當中西流。河南一王屬大寔。河北一王屬突厥所管。土地亦出駞騾羊馬疊布之類。衣著皮裘疊布。食多餅麨。言音各別。不同餘國。不識*仏法。無有寺舍僧尼。〔31 **骨咄國**〕又跋賀那*國東有一國。名骨咄國。此王元是突厥種族。當土百姓。半胡半突厥。土地出駞騾羊馬牛驢蒲桃疊布毛毯之類。衣著疊布皮裘。言音半吐火羅半突厥。半當土。王及首領百姓等*。敬信三寶。有寺有僧行小乘法。此國屬大寔所管。外國雖云道國。共漢地一箇大州相似。此國男女剪鬚髮。女人在髮。〔32 **突厥所住境界**〕又從此胡國已北。〻至北海。西至西海。東至漢國。已*北惣*是突厥所住境界。此等突厥不識仏法。無寺無僧。衣著皮毬氈衫。以虫*爲食。亦無城墎處。氈帳爲屋。行住隨身。隨逐水草。男人並剪鬌髮。女人在頭。言音与諸國不同。國人愛煞。不識善惡。土地足駞騾羊馬之屬。〔33 **胡蜜**〕又從吐火羅國。東行七日。至胡蜜王住城。當來於吐火羅國。逢漢使入蕃。略題四韻取辭。五言 君恨西蕃遠。余嗟東路長。道

1. *Ms. 有. F. 又 H. 有

3. *Ms. 識. F. 知. H. 謝

4. *Ms. 舥. S. 那. F. 舥 H. 那

6. *Ms. 百姓等. F. 百姓大敬 H. 百姓等

8. *Ms. 已北. F. 案慧超以爲骨咄在汗舥之東故云此國已北. 漢國已北. 衍已北二字.

9. *Ms. 惣. F. 總. H. 惣

10. *Ms. 虫. Fuchs. 宍. F. 虫. H. 宍

荒宏雪嶺險澗賊途倡鳥飛驚峭嶷人去偏樑平生不捫淚今日灑千行

冬日在吐火羅逢雪述懷　五言

冷雪牽冰合寒風擘地烈巨海凍墁壇江河凌崖嚙龍門絕瀑布井口盤蛇結伴火上眩歌焉能度播蜜

此胡蜜王兵馬少弱不能自護見屬大寔所管每年輸稅絹三千疋住居山谷處所狹小百姓貧多衣著皮裘氈衫王著綾絹疊布食唯餅麨土地極寒甚於餘國言音與諸國不同所出羊牛極小不大亦有馬騾有僧有寺行小乘法王及首領百姓等總事佛不歸外道所以此國無外道男並剪除鬚髮女人在頭住居山裏其山無有樹木及於百草

又胡蜜國北山裏有九箇識匿國九箇王各領兵馬而住有一箇王屬胡蜜王自外各並自住不屬餘國近有兩窟王來投於漢國使命安西往來絕唯王首領衣著疊布皮裘自餘百姓唯是皮裘氈衫土地極寒為居雪山不同餘國亦有羊馬牛驢言音各別不同諸國

荒宏雪嶺。險澗賊途倡。鳥飛驚峭嶷。人去偏樑雖。平生不捫淚。今日灑千行。
冬。日在吐火羅逢雪述懐。五言　冷雪牽氷合。寒風擘地烈。巨海凍
墁壇。江河凌崖囓。龍門絕瀑布。井口盤虵結。伴火上陔歌。焉能度播
蜜。此胡蜜王。兵馬少弱。不能自護。見屬大寔所管。每年輸稅絹
三千疋。住居山谷。處所狹小。百姓貧多。衣著皮裘氎衫。王著綾絹疊布。
食唯餅飦土地極寒。甚於餘國。言音与諸國不同。所出羊牛。極小不大。
亦有馬騾。有僧有寺。行小乘法。王及首領百姓等。*惣事仏不歸外道。所
以此國無外道。男並剪除鬢髮。女人在頭。住居山裏。其山無有樹水*及於百草。
〔34 識匿國〕又胡蜜國北山裏。有九箇識匿國。九箇王各領兵馬而住。有一箇王。屬
胡蜜王。自外各並自住。不屬餘國。近有兩窟王。來投於漢國使命安
西。往來絕。唯王首領。衣著疊布皮裘。自餘百姓。唯*是皮裘氎衫。
土地*極寒。爲居雪山。不同餘國。亦有羊馬牛驢。言音各別。不同諸國。

T(akakusu)

1. *高楠,
烈慧王林音義作裂.

7. *Ms. 惣. F. 總
H. 惣

8. F. 羅君札記肉云其
山無有樹水. 水殆
木之譌.

11. *Ms. 是. F. 唯皮

12. *Ms. 土地. F. 土.

彼王常遣三二百人於大播蜜川劫彼興胡及於使命縱有絹積
在庫中聽從壞爛亦不解作衣著也此識匿等國云為仙法也
又從胡蜜國東行十五日過播蜜川即至葱嶺鎮此即屬漢兵馬見今鎮
押此即舊日王裴星國境為王背叛走投土蕃然今國界無有百姓外
國人呼云渇飯檀國漢名葱嶺　又從葱嶺步入一月至疏勒外國自
呼名伽師祇離國此亦漢軍馬守捉有寺有僧行小乘法喫肉及葱
韮等土人著疊布衣也　又從疏勒東行一月至龜茲國即是安西
大都護府漢國兵馬大都集處此龜茲國足寺足僧行小乘法食肉及
葱韮等也漢僧行大乘法　又安西南去于闐國二千里亦足漢軍馬
領押足寺足僧行大乘法不食肉也從此已東並是大唐境界諸人共知
不言可悉　開元十五年十一月上旬至安西于時節度大使趙君
且於安西有兩所漢僧住持行大乘法不食肉也大雲寺主秀行善能
講說先是京中七寶臺寺僧　大雲寺都維那名義超善解律藏

1 彼王常遣三二百人於大播蜜川。劫彼與胡及於使命。縱劫得絹。積
2 在庫中。聽從壞爛。亦不解作衣著也。此識匿等國無有仏法也。
3 **〔35 葱領（渴飯檀國）〕** 又從胡蜜國東行十五日。過播蜜川*。卽至葱嶺鎭。此卽屬漢。兵馬見
4 押。此卽舊日王裴星國境。爲王背叛。走投土蕃。然今國界無有百姓。外
5 國人呼云渴飯檀國。漢名葱嶺。**〔36 疎勒〕** 又從葱嶺步入一月。至疏勒。外國自
6 呼名伽師祇離國。此亦漢軍馬守捉。有寺有僧。行小乘法。喫肉及葱
7 韮等。土人著疊布衣也。**〔37 龜兹〕** 又從疏勒東行一月。至龜兹國。卽是安西
8 大都護府。漢國兵馬大都集處。此龜兹國。足寺足僧。行小乘法。食*肉及
9 葱韮等也。漢僧行大乘法。**〔38 于闐〕** 又安西南去于闐國二千里。亦足*漢軍馬
10 領押。足寺足僧。行大乘法。不食肉也。從此已東。並是大唐境界。諸人共知。
11 不言可悉 開元十五年十一月上旬。至安西。于時節度大使趙君。**〔39 安西、大雲寺、龍興寺〕**
12 且於安西。有兩所漢僧住持。行大乘法。不食肉也。大雲寺主秀行善能
13 講說。先是。京*中七寶臺寺僧**。大雲寺都維***舵。名義超善解律藏。舊

3. *Ms. 川？以？

8. *Ms. 食. F. 喫

9. *Ms. 足？是？. F. 是

13. *Ms. 京. F. 市
** 僧, F. □
***Ms. 都維舥

是京中莊嚴寺僧也　大雲寺上座名明惲大有行業亦是京中僧
此等僧大好住持甚有道心樂崇功德　龍興寺主名法海雖是漢兒
生安西學識人風不殊華夏　于闐有一漢寺名龍興寺有一漢僧
是彼寺主大好住持彼僧是河北冀州人士疏勒亦有漢大雲寺有
僧住持即是岷州人士　又從安西東行　至焉耆國是漢軍兵
馬領押有王百姓是胡足寺足僧行小乘法　此即安西四鎮名數
一安西　二于闐　三疏勒　四焉耆
人依漢法裹頭著裙

1 是京中荘嚴寺僧也。大雲寺上座。名明惲。大有行業。亦是京中僧。
2 此等僧。大好住持甚有通心樂崇□*德　龍興寺主。名法海。雖是漢兒
3 生安西。學識人風。不殊華夏。于闐有一漢寺。名龍興寺。有一漢僧。名□□。
4 是彼寺主。大好住持。彼僧是河北冀州人士。疎勒亦有漢大雲寺。有一漢
5 僧住持。卽是崏州人士。〔**40　烏耆國**〕又從安西東行□□至烏*者國。是漢軍兵□**
6 領押。有王。百姓是胡。足寺足僧。行小乘法。□□□□□此卽安西四*鎭名□
7 一安西　二于闐　三疏勒　四烏者　(約十二字缺)(約四字缺)依漢法裹頭著裙(下缺)

2. *Ms. □德, F.H. 功慮, 案慮殆德之譌.

5. *Ms. 烏？焉？, F.H. 焉.
**Ms. 兵□; F. 兵領押.

6. *Ms. 四. F. 山鎭, 案山鎭山字. 殆四之譌. H. 四鎭

INDEX

Abhidharma 12
Airāvatī River 39, 59
Alexander the Great 59
Amoghavajra 16, 19, 33, 35
An-hsi 14–5, 57–8, 73
Arabs 21, 44–5, 52–6
—conquest 71
Arhat
—feeding miracle 46
Asaṅga 49
Ashes
on body 40, 60
Asia
—Central 2, 7, 11, 15, 20–2
25, 54
Aśoka
—tree 42
A-yeh 48

Bāmiyān 51
Bandhana 39
Bhoja 12
Bhramarā 64
Bodhgayā 15, 29
Brahma 42
Bridges 55
Bokhara 54

Calendar
—royal 11
Camels 43–5, 70
—keeper 52
Canton 12, 14
Ceylon 7, 8, 11, 53
Chalukyas 15
—Eastern 64
Ch'ang-an 7–8, 18–9
Chang-yueh 10
Chang-tsi 10
Ch'ien yuan-p'u-t'i
—monastery 19
Chin-ko
—monastery 18–9
Ch'iu-fa kao-seng chuan 12
Chitral 50
Chin-kang-ting-ching Ta-yü-chia Hsin-ti fa-men yi-chüeh 16
Chuang-yen
—monastery 57
Cunningham, Alexander 27–9, 62

Dharmapāla 24
Dharmacakra Saṅghārāma 39, 60
Dragon
—Gate 56, 72
—King 46
—pool 46
Dress 39–58
Durgā 64

Elephants 40–2, 44–6, 49
Ellora 64
Empress Wu 12
Ephthalites
see Huns

Fa-hsien 7–8, 10–2, 20, 25, 28–9
Fa-hai 58
Falcons 41
Fan-wang-ching 16
Feast
—Wu-che 49
Felt 48
—tents 55
Ferghana 54, 72
Fire
—Religion 54
Food 41–2, 44–58
Fuchs, W. 1 ff.
Fu-lin
—Greater 53
—Lesser 53

Gandhāra 9, 25, 48, 50, 68
Geese 43, 65
Gold 41–2, 49, 51, 53
Grapes 46, 49, 52, 66

Han-seng 66
Harṣa 26, 61
Hawks 65
Hīnayāna 40–2, 44, 51
Holy
—places 61
Horses 42–44, 46, 48–50
Houses 41, 46
Hsi-yü chi 11, 13, 36
Hsin-lo
see Silla
Hsüan-tsang 10–3, 20–4, 26, 60
Hsiu–hsing 57
Hu 51–4
—traders 56, 74
Hui-ching 7
Hui-hsiao 19
Hui-lang 19
Hui-li 10
Hui-lin 15, 20, 35
Hui-sheng 9
Hui-wei 7
Hui-ying 7
Huns 25, 62
Hye T'ong 34

I-ching 12–5, 20–4, 28
Images
—Buddha 40, 61
Insects 55, 59, 72

Jālandhara 15, 44
Jetavana 29

Kanauj 11, 15, 61
Kaniṣka 49
Kānyakubja 40
Kao Hsien-chih 21
Kāpiśa 15, 48–51
Kaputana 54
Kashgar 21, 57–8
Kashgiri
see Kashgar
Kaśmīr 15, 25, 36, 44–8, 66
Khmer 15
Khotan 9, 11, 57–8, 73
Khuttal 54
Kish 54
Kittoe, Major 62
K'o-fan-t'an
see Ts'ung Ling
Ko Hsien Chih 66
K'u
—kings 56
Kuang-chou
see Canton
Kucha 11, 15, 57, 75
K'uei-chi 20
Kushan 25
Kuśinagara 7, 15, 34, 39–40

Lampāka 50
Lice 48
Lion
—statue 39
Lung-hsing
—monastery 40

Mahābodhi
—monastery 58
Mahādeva 40, 60
Mahāyāna 3, 40–2, 44
Mahāyāna-yogavajra-prakṛtisāgara-mañjuśrī-sahasrābāhu-sahasrapatra-mahātantrāja-sūtra 15
Maimarg 54, 72
Mañjuśrī 18, 35
Meat
—eating 57

—selling 42
—slaughter 53
Mitra
—monk 35
Monasteries
—building 47
Muslim 21–2, 62, 71

Nagaradhana 45
Nāgārjuna 24, 43
Nālanda 12, 24, 26, 29
Nan-hai Chi-kuei nei-fa chuan 13
Nicobar 15
Nyāyānusārāśāstra 45

Pei-shu 34–5
P'ei-hsing 56
Peking 12
Pelliot, Paul 1, 14, 77
Persia 52
Po-mi Valley 57
Pratyeka Buddha 40, 45
Prison 41, 44
Pure Land 16, 18

Rājagṛha 15, 29
Rājgir
see Rājagṛha
Relic 2, 51, 63, 70
Rhinoceros 39
Rice 41–58
Roman 71

Sadakata, Akira 1
Samarkand 54, 70
Sārnath 7, 15, 29
Sātavāhana 24
Sha-tuo-kan 51
Sheep 41–3, 46
Shignan 73
Shih-lo 54
Shih-ni
—countries 56
Śibi
—king 49, 69
Silk 53, 56
Silla 14, 18
Silver 41–3, 49, 51
Sindhukula 46
Slaves 39, 47, 59
Smith, Vincent 28
Śākra 42, 64
Śrāvasti 42, 63
Stūpa 39–42, 45, 49, 61
Śubhakarasiṃha 19, 34
Sugarcane 49
Sumatra 12
Sung Yün 9, 25
Suvarṇagotra 44
Swāt 9
Szechuan 10

Ta-yün
—monastery 57
T'ai-tsung 10–11
Tajjika
see Arab
Takka 44
Talas River 21
Tamasavana 45
T'ang 57
Tantra 18–9
Tao-ching 29
Tao-hsüan 20
Taoist
—philosophy 2
Ta-hao 9
Ta-po-mi 56
Tibet 21, 44, 47–8
Tiger 39
Tokhāristān 51–2, 54–5
T'o-pa 9
Trāyatriṃśa
—heaven 42, 63
Topes

see *stūpa*
T'si-pao-t'an
—monastery 57
Ts'ung Ling 56–7
Ttōk 67
Tun-huang 1, 9
Turbans 58
Turks 21, 25, 48–54, 71

Udyāna 9, 50
Uposatha 39

Vaiśālī 39
Vajrabodhi 14–5, 19–20
Valabhī 15, 21
Vārānasī 14–5, 39, 60
Vasubandhu 49
Vatapi 64
Vinaya 7, 12–3, 57
—*Mūlasarvāstivadin* 12

Wakhān 55–6
Watters, Thomas 23–4
Wives 47, 54
Wu Chih 58
Wu-t'ai
—Mounain 16, 18–9
Yakṣas 43, 49
Yang-t'ung 49
Yaśovarman 62
Yen Cheng 19
Yogācāra 24
Yüan-chao 20–1
Yu-hua
—monastery 19

Zābulistān 51